MANAGING
VULNERABILITY

Tavistock Clinic Series

Margot Waddell (Series Editor)

Published by Karnac Books

Orders

Tel: +44 (0)20 7431 1075; Fax: +44 (0)20 7435 9076

Email: shop@karnacbooks.com

www.karnacbooks.com

MANAGING VULNERABILITY

The Underlying Dynamics of Systems of Care

Tim Dartington

KARNAC

First published in 2010 by
Karnac Books
118 Finchley Road
London NW3 5HT

British Library Cataloguing in Publication Data

A C.I.P. for this book is available from the British Library

ISBN: 978–1–85575–888–9

Edited, designed, and produced by Communication Crafts

Printed in Great Britain

www.karnacbooks.com

Dedicated to
Eric Miller and Anna Dartington

CONTENTS

II
The survival of the unfittest

III
The personal and the professional

IV
Conclusions

SERIES EDITOR'S PREFACE

Margot Waddell

Since it was founded in 1920, the Tavistock Clinic has developed a wide range of developmental approaches to mental health which have been strongly influenced by the ideas of psychoanalysis. It has also adopted systemic family therapy as a theoretical model and a clinical approach to family problems. The Clinic is now the largest training institution in Britain for mental health, providing postgraduate and qualifying courses in social work, psychology, psychiatry, and child, adolescent, and adult psychotherapy, as well as in nursing and primary care. It trains about 1,700 students each year in over 60 courses.

The Clinic's philosophy aims at promoting therapeutic methods in mental health. Its work is based on the clinical expertise that is also the basis of its consultancy and research activities. The aim of this Series is to make available to the reading public the clinical, theoretical, and research work that is most influential at the Tavistock Clinic. The Series sets out new approaches in the understanding and treatment of psychological disturbance in children, adolescents, and adults, both as individuals and in families.

This fine volume, *Managing Vulnerability*, is essentially about the management of anxiety, both institutional and personal. It is about a moral, social, and political understanding of the relationship between the group and the individual, between society and the self. Based on Tim Dartington's forty years of experience in the field of organizational and managerial consultancy, much of it focused on work and research in health and social care services, the book belongs in the noble tradition of social enquiry that, one way or another, has walked the corridors of the Tavistock for many years.

Dartington takes on major questions and dilemmas, some of the most pressing ones of these times: How do we look after those who cannot look after themselves? How do we marry an understanding of the unconscious, whether in the individual or the group, with public notions of efficiency and effectiveness? What is the nature of change, and how can it be brought about despite resistance? What is a primary task? What is leadership? How can we deal with the long-term dependency of an ageing population?

The book radically questions, from the inside as well as the outside, the current procedure-led and instrumental view of human service provision. It is hard-hitting in its informed and scholarly critique of current theory, policy, and practice. But it is also deeply moving in its personal account of living with this same system while also managing dementia within the family—the early-onset Alzheimer's of Tim Dartington's wife, Anna, whose creative life and mind lit up clinical work at the Tavistock for so many years.

The pages cross conventional boundaries or categorizations of thought, pulling together a broad range of disciplines—systemic, dynamic/psychoanalytic, political, and social care theory—and moving from the broadest circles of public policy to the most intensely private and personal. It is at once profoundly humane and also a constructively angry book—an indictment of what have become the target-led inadequacies and indignities of the care system that have not been expressed before with this degree of accessibility, clarity, experience, and, frankly, wisdom and passion. In this sense it is a trail-blazing book: in many ways shocking, but also authoritative and somehow hopeful. Dartington addresses the theoretical frameworks that certainly buttress caring capacities but can also act as a defence against the proper meaning of "care" and, perhaps most significant of all, its components of compassion and altruism.

As he puts it, "dementia has [become] the disease that is a metaphor for a life destroyed by a malevolent twist of fate." As such, it is a powerful statement about the human condition—reaching far into many of the unexpected recesses of what turn out to be a life's experience. A fitting subtitle could have been, "the heart of the matter": topical, challenging, and reflective, it modestly and movingly engages with what W. R. Bion called "the dark and sombre world of thought".

ABOUT THE AUTHOR

Tim Dartington is a writer and social scientist. He was a researcher at the Tavistock Institute of Human Relations in the 1970s, working with Eric Miller and Isabel Menzies Lyth, and is now an Associate of both the Tavistock Institute and the Tavistock & Portman NHS Foundation Trust. He is a member of OPUS (an Organisation for Promoting Understanding of Society) and ISPSO (the International Society for the Psychoanalytic Study of Organizations). He continues to carry out consultancy and research for a wide range of organizations from a systems psychodynamic perspective and has written on organizational issues in the public and not-for-profit sectors. He has also written for radio and the theatre.

ACKNOWLEDGEMENTS

My debt to my family, to Dan and Jake, and to friends goes way beyond the scope of this book. Thank you all.

This is also the product of conversations with many people, too numerous to list, including students at the Tavistock Clinic, especially those who contributed to the Consultation and Organisation (D10) theory lectures and seminars for the Professional Doctorate in Social Work (D60); also colleagues at the Policy Seminars of the Tavistock and Portman NHS Trust; and participants in the "refresh programme" of the Tavistock Institute.

I presented earlier versions of some sections at conferences for the Tavistock Institute and OPUS (an Organisation for Promoting Understanding of Society) and at a policy seminar of the Tavistock Clinic, in London; at an ESRC (Economic and Social Research Council) seminar hosted by the Open University in Milton Keynes; and at the ISPSO (International Society for the Psychoanalytic Study of Organizations) conference in Toledo, Spain. I thank Mannie Sher and Eliat Aram, Lionel Stapley, Andrew Cooper, Jessica Evans, and Manuel Seijo, for these opportunities; and all those who heard and commented on these papers as work in progress.

I have also drawn on earlier publications: in particular, articles in the journals *Sociology of Health Illness* (1979), *Dementia* (2007), and the *British Medical Journal* (2008). Anna Dartington's chapter, "My Unfaithful Brain", was first published in *Looking into Later Life: A Psychoanalytic Approach to Depression and Dementia in Old Age* (ed. R. Davenhill, 2007), also in the Tavistock Clinic series.

* * *

Here is a short selection of those who have helped me greatly, whether they knew it or not:

Gabriella Braun, Francesca Cardona, Nancy Cohn, Andrew Cooper, Rachael Davenhill, Miranda Feuchtwang, Stephan Feuchtwang, Angela Foster, Jonathan Gosling, Susanne Gosling, Cheryl Holman, Charlotte Jarvis, John Keady, Olya Khaleelee, Sebastian Kraemer, James Krantz, Gordon Lawrence, Julian Lousada, Lynn Malloy, Julienne Meyer, Deirdre Moylan, Jean Neumann, Caroline Nicholson, Janet Novak, Christopher Penfold, Bernard Roberts, Sandy Robertson, Michael Rustin, Elizabeth Sampson, Josephine Seccombe, David Towell, Amal Treacher, Margot Waddell.

PREFACE

Three years ago I wrote the editorial to an issue of the journal *Dementia* with the same title as this book, "Managing Vulnerability". I concluded with a question: *What are the conditions in which it is possible and acceptable to be vulnerable in our society and survive?* This book is my contribution to addressing that question at a time of continuing uncertainties in local and global economic and political life.

In fact, this book has some of the characteristics of a journey that goes back longer.

There has been considerable progress in the last forty years in the delivery of care services—for example, in the field of disability—to a great extent through the efforts of people with disabilities themselves. Institutional care, where it still exists, is subject to continuing review, whereas "care in the community" has gone through a succession of policy transformations, with increasing emphasis on person-centred care and now individual budgets and personalization of services. Even Alzheimer's Disease—the most recalcitrant of illnesses to modern medical science—is receiving much greater attention than before, with media interest, celebrity involvement, and the UK government's publication of a dementia care strategy. At the same time, I would argue that there are significant ways in which the world has got tougher for the most vulnerable in our society. A culture of enterprise and opportunity, put to good use by the disabled people's movement, does have a downside: a wide-ranging lack of respect for dependency, even where this is necessary and appropriate, in human relationships. The culture of targets and audit in the delivery of public services—a distortion of organizational theory developed in other sectors—has made the effective delivery of humane and responsive care more difficult to achieve and maintain.

In Part I, I describe in the first chapter how my work over forty years has followed the changes that we have seen to institutional and community care in different contexts, and through the first part of the book I explore my developing awareness of a systems psychodynamics approach to understanding the management of care. Part II illustrates these themes with a more detailed description of the characteristics of care systems.

In Part III, there is a detailed case study of what happened when a member of my own family developed dementia. Kurt Lewin famously said that there was nothing as useful as a good theory—but now life was overtaking my theoretical understanding of the issues.

What is the usefulness of theory? Much is made these days of evidence and the need for an "evidence base" for action. The action research projects that I draw on in Part II were funded by the Department of Health, but such research does not fit easily with the processes required of the National Institute of Health Research (NIHR) Service Delivery and Organisation (SDO) programme that is now in place. This recognizes the importance of good research that evaluates the effectiveness of what is done on our behalf and is paid for out of general taxation. However, there are research methodologies that look for a different level of evidence and are more experiential in their approach. We speak commonly of the evidence of our eyes, or of a gut feeling, as we experience for ourselves the effects of different phenomena. This evidence is too important to be discarded. The action research methodology that brings together an appreciation of systems of organization and a psychodynamic understanding of the underlying motivations affecting how we work together is a way of looking at what can be learned from a position of lived experience.

So the book progresses from a theoretical perspective, to one of action research and consultancy, to the day-by-day experience of a family facing the universal challenges associated with debility, dying, and death.

The book has been created out of these three perspectives. Of course, the reader does not have to take them in that order if, like me, you often prefer to read the end of a book first.

Why bother to write and for you to read this book? Someone told me once that you can tell about a society by the way it looks after its old people. The observation has stayed with me, and it seems as good a test as any. The mother gives birth: the child lives to see the mother grow old and die. We often think that it is a tragedy if it does not work out like that. The care of the elderly requires certain virtues if it is to be done well: patience and generosity, a capacity for empathy and compassion; love, even. There are common areas of kindness to do with kin in relation to any sickness or disability, or a terminal illness. These are virtues in the ancient sense that they follow naturally if certain roles in the family and the wider community are to be taken up fully in our society (MacIntyre, 1981).

In this book I describe ways that systems of care encourage or inhibit the natural processes of compassion and care that make all the difference to our everyday experiences of vulnerability at different stages in our lives, from childhood to old age. I argue that an over-determined approach can be counter-productive if frameworks and standards get in the way of ordinary reactions and responses to need.

There is much that is personal in this book, which purports to be a contribution to social science, especially in Part III, which has the title, "The Personal and the Professional". A part of my motivation has been that I can say things, and describe experiences relevant to our understanding of systems of care, that most researchers—even if they have the skills to observe them—would have to be silent about. Considerations of confidentiality and the strictures of the ethics committee leave them speechless about much that is important to say.

I am somewhat free of these constraints, though not of the ethical considerations: living with someone with dementia has meant facing a long and complex succession of ethical questions in representing the thinking, and the interests that can no longer be articulated directly, of another person.

It is not unusual for social scientists to include themselves as characters in their books. I take comfort from some that I have read and learned much from—Theodore Zeldin (1994), Richard Sennett (1998), Paul Hoggett (1992), among others. Also there have been accounts of illness that could only have been written from the inside. An example is that of my wife, Anna: her chapter "My Unfaithful Brain", reprinted in this volume, was first published in Rachael Davenhill's book *Looking into Later Life* (2007a). Another contribution to that book was by Ronald Markillie (2007), a retired psychoanalyst drawing on his experience of his own analysis fifty years previously in encountering dependency in old age.

I think also of Gillian Rose and her account among many other things of her colostomy—"Thus, I handle shit"—in *Love's Work* (1985). She also includes a quotation from Alexander Herzen, *My Past and Thoughts* (1924), which is relevant to me:

Who is entitled to write his reminiscences?
Everyone. Because no one is obliged to read them.

Naturally I hope this book has a readership, because none of us exists in isolation but only in relation to others. If it is said that a person with dementia is in danger of losing identity through the diminution of his or her contact with others, it follows that the reverse may also become true: living with someone with dementia, does one lose a part of one's own identity? At the least, I can say one feels at risk of losing that identity. This in part explains why we are so disturbed when the person with dementia fails to recognize us: it is as if *we* do not exist. So another explanation for writing this book may well be my own need for reassurance of my identity: readers of this book, who have the curiosity to investigate the underlying processes by which we manage our vulnerability in our private and public lives, will be helping me in this.

Finally, I have to acknowledge the two people to whom this book is dedicated and without whose lives and example it could not have been written: Eric Miller and Anna Dartington.

In 1996 they last worked together as director and associate director of the "Leicester Conference", the international experiential two-week group relations conference that is sponsored by the Tavistock Institute every year at Leicester University. The theme of these conferences is authority and leadership, with an increasing emphasis on role and task and the management of risk in contemporary organizational life. Eric gave me the opportunity to work with him and colleagues at the Tavistock Institute and introduced me to systems psychodynamic thinking about the individual, group, and organization, which has informed all my work. The importance of Anna in my life is beyond words, but reading this book may give you some idea. The influence of these two people on my thinking about the causes and conditions of vulnerability will also be apparent throughout.

Tim Dartington
London, March 2010

PART I

INDIVIDUAL SURVIVAL
AND ORGANIZATIONAL LIFE

CHAPTER ONE

Thinking about systems of care

Can I see another's woe,
And not be in sorrow too?

William Blake

S ystems of care around vulnerable people are subject to pervasive dynamics of integration and fragmentation, as they address contradictory pressures for positive intervention in a context of dependency. They fit uneasily with conventional measures of efficiency and effectiveness, with a contemporary urgency to demonstrate productivity, and their association with societal issues in the face of morbidity and death leaves them exposed to ambivalent attitudes of respect and despair in their development and management.

I have worked as a researcher and consultant with different systems of care over a period of forty years and have observed the effects of these dynamics on the delivery of services to older people, to people with learning difficulties and physical disabilities, and to children. In this time I have come to the view that a sensitive and clear-headed understanding of the underlying contradictions in what they are being asked to do is necessary to allow for the development and maintenance of good practice and the avoidance of abuse.

In developing this argument, my work as a social scientist has been influenced by the systems psychodynamic approach to the understanding of groups and organizations associated with Eric Miller and colleagues at the Tavistock Institute in the 1970s and subsequently, in association with the Tavistock Institute and its group relations programme, with the Tavistock Clinic, and as a member of OPUS—an Organisation for Promoting Understanding of Society.

Much has changed in the NHS over the intervening years, but many of the issues remain disturbingly familiar. In some ways it has been argued that the situation has got worse, "a malignancy of thought" in the provision of long-term care and help for people in later life (Davenhill, 2007b, p. 204). For example, there continues to be a pervasive underlying dynamic in health and social welfare systems providing services to vulnerable people of fragmentation between these health and social services, and this is replicated within and between different health and social welfare agencies across public, private, and voluntary sectors in a mixed economy of care. Why is there this fragmentation? Is it that the task is, in a societal sense, too difficult? Too much associated with failure? Is meeting the dependency needs of vulnerable people to be understood, even when it is done well, as a failure of services to meet targets that are affirmative about opportunity and defensive against the realities of morbidity?

In the 1970s I worked with Eric Miller and colleagues on a Department of Health-funded project on geriatric hospital care. This action research study followed an earlier Tavistock Institute study on institutional systems of care to do with physical disability and was much influenced by that work. I also worked on two other action research studies—of institutional care in a mental handicap hospital, and of the psychological needs of young children in an orthopaedic hospital, a project directed by Isabel Menzies (later Menzies Lyth). I was later involved with a further action research study of systems of care for people with physical impairments living in community settings and was the main author of a report for the Department of Health and of its subsequent publication (Dartington, Miller, & Gwynne, 1981).

Collectively these studies of systems of care of the young and the old, and of mental and physical disability, used an open systems model to explore the relationship of institutional care to the societal environment. Thus, ambivalent attitudes towards an increasingly elderly population were expressed in the relationships of different professionals in the hospital system as well in relation to the families of patients living in the community. The young children in hospital were subjected to indiscriminate caregiving that used them as objects for the expression of adult needs for affection, while the pain and suffering associated with the hospital admission was denied. Later action research studies and consultancy were opportunities to explore these dynamics in the less bounded setting of community-based services. The conflicting pressures to integrate and also to fragment services around vulnerable people were again ways to alleviate the despair associated with intractable and chronic problems associated with the dependency consequent on chronic and degenerative illness (Dartington, 1979).

From group relations thinking, I have wanted to apply the distinctive categorizations of "organization" and "institution" to systems of care. It has been policy to shut down institutions, in the traditional sense of their being closed systems or asylums, and I explored this shift to community care in the 1970s, with further studies of community-based systems around people living with physical disabilities (Dartington, Miller, & Gwynne, 1981).

These new projects successfully combated the isolation and the limitations on ordinary freedoms associated with institutional care. At the same time, as a researcher I became aware of a "disability identity" and suggested this was also important for those who were now able to assert their independence in life choices, where their integration in the community also involved an assertion of difference. In this way I was looking for a third position from that of the warehousing and horticultural models, which had been described previously in the Tavistock studies (Miller & Gwynne, 1972).

In the geriatric hospital study I had followed up a cohort of twenty patients as they were admitted to the hospital. This included interviewing the families from which the patients had come. This aspect of the research furthered my understanding of the motivation and stress of family members in responding to the needs of their elderly relatives (Dartington, 1980).

I then carried out a further study of the inter-agency relations to do with services for elderly mentally infirm people (Dartington, 1986). My hypothesis was that the intractable problems associated with dependency in old age were experienced as too much for one agency to take on as its primary activity—but that a collective effort was being attempted by different agencies. There were people for whom this was their primary focus; but it was not the primary task for their agencies. This led me to consider collaboration as essentially deviant at a systemic level, but common sense at the level of the enthused practitioner.

I pursued this approach further through a series of workshops on collaboration in community care. The experiential evidence was that collaboration, if it was to be effective, was mostly preparation and that only after a long period of planning and inter-agency learning was there likely to be effective engagement. Furthermore, when it does work, this is because those committed to the project are prepared to become deviant to their own organization's primary activity. This is a dynamic that I am also familiar with from Tavistock group relations conferences, where inter-group events involve representation from a base group and also the taking of authority in relation to an emerging issue.

Influenced by Eric Miller, I worked as a consultant to Tavistock small study groups, where the focus of the experiential task of working with the here-and-now of the group was opened up to include a more active awareness of how external influences could affect the inner life of the group. Miller developed a hypothesis in his organizational consultancy and later in OPUS about the small group as a microcosm of the wider system; I continued to work with this methodology in group relations conferences (I was director of the "Leicester Conference" on Authority, Leadership and Organization in 1999 and 2001), in consultancy, and in my work with OPUS in developing its listening posts and study days. The insights from this work informed my view of the individual in society—the OPUS concept of the reflective citizen—and this further informed my understanding of vulnerability and identity (Dartington, 2001).

I have always been interested in managing by enthusiasms (Bishop & Hoggett, 1986), because of the emphasis on authority coming from the task, without undue reliance on structures and procedures and protocols. My work with voluntary organizations (I was head of the Management Development Unit of the National Council for Voluntary Organisations from 1986 to 1994) put me in touch with many organizations founded by people whose lives had been affected by serious illness, trauma, or debility in themselves or in other family members. My consultancy gave me opportunities to observe the dynamics of such organizations—in particular, the nature of the conflicts that emerged within and between staff and trustees (the committee members) and volunteers in such organizations (Dartington, 1996, 1998).

In thinking about vulnerable people in society, it was also necessary to examine from a systems psychodynamic perspective the rational economic model of human relations, which has gained primacy in policy and practice in health and social welfare, as well as in other aspects of the social economy (Dartington, 2004).

Having seen how enthusiasm is necessary, even within formal bureaucratic systems, in order to achieve significant results that were not primary to that organization's immediate objectives, I then encountered at first hand what happens to the individual in an informal system of care, when I also experienced having a family member develop a debilitating illness. Exploring a narrative methodology, I have written about my experience of then living with someone with dementia, and also about the dynamics of palliative care for someone dying at home (Dartington, 2007, 2008) The bringing together of my previous research and the immediate experience of living with someone through successive phases of increasing dependency was also an opportunity (if that is the word) for informal action research on the dynamics—psychological and systemic—of managing vulnerability.

In my work I take a systems psychodynamic approach to thinking about the dynamics of care in health and social welfare agencies, This is "a way of thinking about energizing or motivating forces resulting from the interconnection between various groups and sub-units of a social system" (Neumann, 1999), and, as applied to the understanding of organizations of all kinds and human service organizations in particular, it demands a certain integration of open systems theory with a psychodynamic understanding of individuals and groups in society—easier said than done.

Systems theory takes a scientific approach to the proposition that the whole is greater than the sum of its parts. Meaning is found in the connectedness and interdependence of apparently discrete and separate experiences and actions, and therefore of different structures, concepts, and meanings. The concept of an "open" system draws attention to the relationship of a system to its environment. A system is thought to have a permeable boundary, through which it interacts with the outside world. It receives inputs from its environment, processes them in various ways, and produces outputs. A system thus survives and thrives according to its success in this import–export business.

In this very general sense we may think of a person as a system, managing oneself in relation to the world we live in. We can also apply this template for understanding to large and complex systems, like hospitals or multinational companies.

A "closed" system, in contrast, would be self-contained and interact only with itself. Sometimes organizations may be thought to act as if they are closed systems, not having to bother with external relations. For this reason they may also be thought to have a tendency to deteriorate and run down.

A systemic approach to the understanding of groups and organizations therefore emphasizes the interdependence of all those working in the system. Making an intervention in one part of the system has an impact on other parts. This helps us to understand how there may be resistance to change, but—rather like referred pain—not always where we would expect it.

A system also has a recognizable boundary. This boundary cannot be entirely arbitrary, though it may at times be controversial in what it includes or excludes—much like territorial boundaries. There are bounded (sub-)systems within systems, and the systems that we are aware of are themselves a part of wider systems. Thinking in this way therefore allows us to move between microscopic and macroscopic perspectives on what we are observing and experiencing. This is one of the strengths of thinking systemically, and I would emphasize here that the concept of system as applied to human organization is an exploratory or heuristic device—a useful way of ordering reality at a certain time and place; this is not the same as seeing the world as a complex series of fixed or stable interlocking machines, though we often act as if that is what we think.

The concept of boundary draws attention to the need for there to be management of a system, however it gets defined, so that there is mediation of the transactions that take place between what is inside and outside the system. In the individual, seen as a system, this management may be thought of in terms of ego function. The individual has to understand and manage the boundary between his or her own inner world and the realities of the external environment. In enterprises of different kinds, there is a need also for their management to provide the boundary conditions necessary to carrying out the task, the conversion process that is necessary for the system to do well in practical, social, psychological, and economic terms.

The concept of the open system is attributed to a biologist, Ludwig von Bertalanffy, writing from the perspective of the natural sciences and wanting to make connections between different scientific disciplines (Bertalanffy, 1950). His general systems theory was taken up by social scientists who wanted to think of organizations as more than their technology, seeing people not as inefficient cogs, nor as groups of people acting without reference to the technology. It was open systems theory that led them to a socio-technical understanding of work enterprises, with recognition of the interaction of the human and technical aspects of an enterprise (Miller & Rice, 1967).

Later systemic descriptions also make a distinction between the operating and the management or maintenance systems in the conversion process. These may be seen to be interdependent, each impacting on the other—a dynamic that may be observed, for example, in the relations between professional and managerial leadership in human service organizations.

Another strand of thinking that has been influential in considering how we organize ourselves in different contexts derives from systemic family therapy, which puts an emphasis on the interaction among different family members and seeks to intervene in a way that draws attention to this internal dynamic. It proposes that the family is operating according to implicit rules, in order to maintain homeostasis in relation to external pressures. One of the rules that is always present is that these rules cannot be challenged (Campbell, Draper, & Huffington, 1991). In this way the meaning that those in a system put on a problem facing the enterprise gives an insight into what can be thought about and what cannot. From this perspective it is by reframing the problem that the system has the capacity to transform itself and make changes to its internal structures. A paradoxical injunction involves identifying a behaviour that is symptomatic of what is dysfunctional in the family system and then encouraging that very behaviour. This is intended to make an involuntary symptom into a conscious choice, which can then be rejected. Systemic approaches to consultation to an organization are also intended to make such reframing possible. This is done, for example, by using the consultancy relationship for mutual feedback and the development of alternative hypotheses about the meaning that informs actions. Circular questioning, which focuses on the patterns of connectedness between people, beliefs, and actions, is different from the kind of diagnostic questioning that is looking for a root cause of difficulty or dysfunction. Change in itself is not thought to be the problem; instead there is work to be done on the meanings that change may have for relationships between people and the pressures it puts on their existing rules of engagement.

Although systemic and psychodynamic thinking about the family and other groups are sometimes seen as very different, with different therapeutic trainings and loyalties, it would be in the spirit of systems theory to explore the interrelatedness of these conceptual traditions, and this is attempted, for example, in the "Tavistock" model of group relations training (Miller, 1989).

A psychodynamic understanding of organizations has its starting point in the learning we can achieve about the inner world and unconscious dynamics of the individual affecting his or her interactions with others, and the way we experience these interactions. For this we draw on the insights of psychoanalytic thinking, in particular from the object relations theory of Melanie Klein and others in the British school of psychoanalysis. It is because of the emphasis this gives to the understanding of human relations, rather than the emphasis on instincts in the individual in ego psychology, that post-Kleinian psychoanalytic thinking has been so important in its application to the understanding of human organizations (Armstrong, 2005; Gabriel, 1999; Gould, Stapley, & Stein, 2001; Hinshelwood & Skogstad, 2000; Lawrence, 2000; Obholzer & Roberts, 1994).

This understanding of the individual, the human element in the equation, has to be put alongside two other focal points for considering how organizations are the way they are, and these have to do with task and technology. The approach draws on the pioneering work of the social scientists at the Tavistock Institute incorporating psychoanalytic concepts with other disciplines after the Second World War. They included psychiatrists, psychologists, and others, who had addressed issues of leadership in the selection of officers and the dynamics of groups in the rehabilitation of soldiers from the trauma of their war experience. In doing this they were also influenced by Kurt Lewin (1947) to think in a holistic way about the dynamics of groups and organizations. By considering the interaction of the human element with the machinery of production or service delivery, they developed a socio-technical approach to thinking about the workplace, using their consultancy practice as a way of researching aspects of work organization, for example in coalmining (Trist & Bamforth, 1951) and engineering (Jaques, 1951). Rice and Miller developed and tested their open systems model of consultancy with textile mills in India (Miller, 1975; Rice, 1958). Menzies Lyth (1960) is remembered in particular for her study of nursing. The concept of task is crucial to seeing an organization as an open system, interacting with its environment; Miller and Rice (1967) developed a practice-based conceptual base for what has come to be known as a systems psychodynamic view of organizational life.

The psychoanalytic thinking that informs this work has led to an analysis of organizational defences, most famously in the work of Menzies, and is concerned primarily with understanding the nature of anxiety. We all have some awareness of a primitive anxiety, an ever-present all-pervasive anxiety that is part of the human condition. This is a dread of the unknown, the child's fear of the dark, of annihilation. We may think of the rituals, the totems and taboos, in primitive society that Freud (1912–13) described as ways of coping with this dread. There are other ways of managing anxiety in our own world, including the institutional structures that give us some security.

Workplace institutions serve some of the purposes of traditional social groupings. The psychiatrist and psychoanalyst Wilfred Bion identified the old triumvirate of Church, looking after our dependency needs; Army, our predilection for fight, or if we can't fight, then flight; and Aristocracy, providing a model of well-bred achievement (Bion, 1961). But these three social institutions providing defence mechanisms against such primitive anxiety are no longer in charge. In today's context, fight–flight is the organizational valency of enterprises in a sink-or-swim market economy; dependency may still be the appropriate valency for a public sector organization (who may have to look after the unenterprising in an enterprise culture); and the voluntary sector, with its record of innovation and partnership, has given new energy to the great and good, who have continued through the honours system and the House of Lords to represent an evolving aristocracy of our times (Dartington, 1998). At the same time we have seen some of the serious side-effects of a market economy, with a public sector espousing the competitiveness of the private sector, and a voluntary sector that increasingly conforms to both private and public sector norms of organizational identity.

Theory can be useful in this context in thinking about vulnerability. We recognize the anxiety that the individual may experience because of early experience of loss and the tendency of the individual to respond to stressful situations in a certain way. Melanie Klein was able to think about this because of her unflinching look at the despair that the child faces. If Freud discovered the sexuality behind the innocent form, Klein (1945) discovered violence, hate, destructiveness, and—just as important—the need, therefore, for means of reparation.

Of course, work itself brings its own anxieties and the institution defends against these specific anxieties. For example, nursing involves the transgression of many taboos to do with privacy, sexuality, and nakedness as well as primitive anxieties about death and dying. We learn to cope with these primitive anxieties and to defend against them in functional and sometimes dysfunctional ways. Klein describes the way we learn to recognize that things are not all good or all bad but contain elements of both, of what we want to possess and what we want to reject. Her description of what then came to be called the depressive position can be put alongside the work of others in describing the conditions for what Bion (1962), for example, called containment and reverie and Donald Winnicott (1965) called the holding environment. Processes of splitting and projection remain a way we seek to organize our psychic experience and also become apparent in the organizations we live and work in. So psychoanalysts Jaques and Menzies, undertaking consultation to social systems, to organizations with employers and employees, found that the same mechanisms were at work and that working relations in organizations are deeply influenced by the unconscious anxieties of their members (Jaques, 1955; Menzies Lyth, 1960).

In summary, this is the tradition of social enquiry that I am now wanting to apply to one of the demographic challenges of contemporary society. The Tavistock Institute brought together a group of social scientists in a time of post-war reconstruction. The welfare state in its post-war origins was expected to stabilize and develop an equilibrium in meeting the health and social security needs of a society at peace with itself. Successes in, for example, facing down the incidence of cancers and heart disease have left an ageing population increasingly exposed to long-term conditions of dependency. Social policy has now promoted a post-dependency culture of opportunity, individualism, and enterprise, but how do we look after those who cannot look after themselves? As a society, we have to recognize that we are not very good at it. And, to face this challenge, it would help to acknowledge and understand more the underlying processes that make the status of vulnerable people so problematic in the systems of care that are supposed to be addressing that vulnerability.

CHAPTER TWO

The gang in the organization

And now, what will become of us without barbarians?
They were a kind of solution.

C. P. Cavafy

Why bother to understand unconscious processes in organizations? In a sense this question is a critique of an increasingly instrumental view of human service organizations, as they have been influenced by business schools and accountancy-led consultancies in meeting government policy directives. At times it seems that we have returned to a Taylorian view of organization as a factory (Taylor, 1947), with a production line of protocols and algorithms to ensure conformity and quality control according to certain specifications, frameworks, and standards. The assumption is that we just have to get the procedures right and the enterprise will work efficiently. The example of failures in child protection has exposed some of the limitations of this approach. Protocols and standards are helpful and necessary, but they are not sufficient. Alongside these mechanisms, we have to give serious attention to unconscious processes that are endemic to the dynamics of group and organizational life—and that are sometimes supportive of an organizational task, and sometimes not.

Those who manage organizations have to be defended to some extent against uncertainty—otherwise they would be overwhelmed—but it seems to me that omnipotence can then get out of hand. When it does, we see what I would describe as the gang in the organization, a kind of narcissistic leadership (and followership) that acts as if there is a fusion between the self and the desired object: if I get my way, everything will be all right; if my view of the world goes unchallenged, everything will be for the best in the best of all possible worlds. A capacity for thinking is dangerous to such a polarized view, so we should look to see how we may all at times tend to set up situations at work that are not conducive to thinking.

At the Tavistock Institute, Miller and Rice (1967) showed how we can link our understanding of the individual to that of the group and the organization:

> The individual, the small group, and the larger group are seen as progressively more complex manifestations of a basic structural principle. Each can be described in terms of an internal world, an external environment, and a boundary function which controls transactions between what is inside and what outside. [p. 15]

Management can be seen in terms of the ego function. In the individual:

> The ego—the concept of the self as a unique individual—mediates the relationships between the internal world of good and bad objects and the external world of reality, and thus takes, in relation to the personality, a "leadership" role. [p. 16]

How does this relate to management?

> The members of an enterprise depend on their managers to identify their tasks and provide the resources for task performance. A manager who fails, or even falters, as inevitably he sometimes must, deprives his subordinates of satisfaction and thereby earns their hatred. But the leadership role of management is a lonely role and leaders must have followers; any

hanging back or turning away is a threat to their own ful-
filment. This inevitable, and mutual, dependence, increases
their need of both leaders and followers to defend themselves
against the destructive power of their potential hostility to each
other. [p. 17]

One advantage of thinking in terms of open systems—of inputs
to an enterprise, a conversion process, and then outputs back in
to the environment—is that we can track the different inputs and
the varied transitions that take place in complex systems. In the
management of the care of vulnerable people, because of the dependency within the system, we have to be specially alert to these
psychological defences and the ways that hostility get expressed
or displaced in what we may find to be anti-task activity in the
organization.

One characteristic of leadership concerns achieving shared
meaning among those involved in any enterprise. In hospitals,
you can see differences in perception of task between doctors and
nurses; among nurses in different wards but working with the
same patients; and between all of them and the other professionals,
and the patients and their families. We are not just talking about
difference—of course we are all different and have different things
to do.

In my research with health and social care agencies, I was observing in addition a destructive process of psychological splitting,
so that not far below the surface the difference leads to a breakdown of shared meaning: what you are doing is deviant from what
I am doing; I've got it right, you've got it wrong. Also, this process
may go largely unnoticed, except by the patient who experiences a
kind of Alice in Wonderland world of changing identity according
to all these different perceptions.

There is a wider organizational context. We have been much
taken with issues of the post-dependency culture associated with
the policy critique of professional and institutional oligarchies and
the metaphor of the market. At the same time ethics and public
relations become fused (Evans, 2009). What is important is how
you organize your narcissistic defences. Reality is how you present
the facts—so that what is factual becomes itself a matter for negotiation.

In such a societal context, we are more easily able to identify perverse forms of management (Long, 2008). Much goes unre-marked, as we have got used to an image of managers as omnipo-tent infants. There used to be an advertisement for business-class passengers on trans-Atlantic flights: "It's tough at the top but nice and comfy round the bottom." There has been a long tradition of the executive bathroom, but what we were now being asked to accept was a primitive and indulgent image of the comforts of financial reward—managers in nappies.

In the voluntary sector, where charities are expected to meet criteria of public good, over forty years we have seen managers metamorphose from coordinator (in small organizations) or gen-eral secretary (in larger organizations) to director (managing half a dozen people) and now chief executive. The emphasis has moved from facilitation to control to decision-making. But in that process an aspect of leadership to do with not-knowing has to be denied or defended against—and that is a task for the gang mentality in the organization, which drives out thought and is prepared to pay a high price for certainty.

Nevertheless, we are, as always, in a world of multiple stake-holders. The inquiry into *Tomorrow's Company* carried out by the Royal Society of Arts (1995) explored the implications, as if this were new land to be discovered, that companies have to take ac-count of stakeholders other than shareholders. In the voluntary sector, the question of ownership of the organization has remained subtle and resistant to quick fixes. What is still less easily recog-nized by those who hanker after a simple model of leadership from the top (in the monotheistic tradition of our dominant religions) is that stakeholders are not integrative by instinct. Their interests are very often not the same. Nor is an organization to be under-stood—however corporate its image—as a single organism, like a primitive life form.

The post-dependent culture has seen the emergence of a quasi-fundamentalism in organizational life, with an emphasis on cor-poratism but without loyalty. The impact within organizations has been far-reaching, affecting the capacity of the individual to act with personal authority.

From the 1980s, organizational consultants were selling mission statements like medieval mendicants in order to absolve organ-izational sins. People worked increasingly with fundamentalist intensity but without any real expectation of a relaxed and fulfilling future existence. Instead, especially in the public sector, they became embroiled in a frenetic response to a virtual reality imposed from somewhere outside their experience: personal authority gave way to public audit, and this had a particularly numbing effect on the capacity of systems of care to do their job.

From a psychoanalytic perspective, in thinking about organizations, we have long been aware of a tension between task and anti-task in the unconscious processes that affect the efficiency and effectiveness of an enterprise—for example, Isabel Menzies Lyth, with reference to adolescent institutions, where she argued that the education system is not working for preparedness for life in society but for dependency needs that are anti-maturational (Menzies Lyth, 1979).

My hypothesis is that these unconscious dynamics are not perverse exceptions, to be isolated and dealt with severely by "special measures" . I want to think how the sabotage of the task is itself endemic to the culture of organizations. The question is not, how do we do away with it, but how do we understand and live with it?

We have to think what we mean when we talk of group unconscious processes. I find useful the experiential learning of group relations conferences with the theme of authority and leadership. I would define a group by the evidence of people being prepared to engage with each other, to share in the collective emotional life of the group. An example that is familiar to all of us is that of the theatre audience. The hush as the lights go down is a moment of collective anticipation. It is not as exciting in everyday life and work, but some quality of anticipation is below the surface of any meeting where there is real work going on.

We may think also how the common awareness of a problem or a crisis of any kind will bring an aggregate of individuals into collective identity, with shared fantasies of potential disaster and hope of salvation. The basic assumptions identified by Bion therefore may be thought even to define the group. They are evidence of a group identity at work in the unconscious of members of the group. This is not saying that there is a group mind, separate from and distinct from the states of mind of the individuals in the group.

The individuals create the group and not the other way round. Or, with reference to Bion's theory of thinking, we may consider the group as a thought waiting to be discovered by its members.

The exercising of group membership is more like the easily observable physical phenomenon of two people walking together: not touching, but without conscious awareness or effort, they are walking in step. We can think of more complex examples of group membership leading to remarkable uniformity—for example, where the menstrual cycles of women in total institutions also develop a common rhythm.

The individual in a group is not autonomous in psychological as well as physiological reactions to stimuli external and internal to the group, and in the context of a group relations conference we see how readily we create a group culture that meets our primitive needs for security and nurturing.

This group culture will at times express both paranoid-schizoid and depressive characteristics. Different members of the group— and different parts of an organization—will express different aspects of the unconscious processes as they affect the work task. The purchaser–provider relationship is interesting in this context— a separation of powers is not simply an efficient mobilization of market forces but an acknowledgement of a primitive struggle for dominance in our object relations. It provides an effective vehicle for projective identification and for vilification of those we love to hate because they remind us of our dependence and so threaten our omnipotent defences.

In a group relations event, I saw the coming together of a group that took on the characteristics of a gang.

There were ten people in the group. (There were ten staff in the conference. It is not unusual for a group to mirror the management and then parody its worst features.) They had formed from a sub-set of the members and included several people who had other significant relationships in their work roles outside the conference.

At first two women, working together, led the group into a culture of solidarity. They stated without fear of contradiction that there would be no conflict in the group. The task (in the conference) was to interact with other groups, so they said they would interact. The context of the interaction apparently did not matter. They would present themselves to the outside world as undifferentiated and would support each other whatever happened. (In my observation, they were so much under the influence of unconscious processes that they were without a morality. The management had asked them to carry out an activity. They then acted as a management without a conscience.)

They went to meet another group, about which they knew nothing, chosen at random. This group declined to meet with them *en masse*. Thwarted in their immediate aim, they reacted by taking a hostage. They returned triumphant, crowing over their success.

What was striking was that they had no sense of an ethical question that might arise from their conduct. The impact of their behaviour on another group was a matter of no concern to them. They felt that they now had an identity, and that was the important thing for them. They repeated the oldest justification for all unacknowledged cruelty, that the ends justify the means. The cruelty was unacknowledged because their anger was unacknowledged. The totalitarian atmosphere in the group was very hard to bear.

A black man in this otherwise white group expressed some doubts about how they had related to other groups. "Why didn't you leave, then?" was the immediate response from one of the leader women. The only way of dealing with dissent was to get rid of it.

Later, the two women became increasingly preoccupied with the distress of another member of the other group, from which they had taken a hostage. They now thought to offer a merger of the two groups—that is, complete fusion.

The two women, who clearly were acting as the leaders of a group that they claimed was leaderless, were from social services and the ambulance service. Who would dare to challenge their aggressive intent? The anxiety they imported into the system was then turned into an unattributable attack on the conference management.

In such group relations work, we can observe some common examples of sabotage of thinking. For example, within a group, a certain proposition may be considered generally applicable. ("The group is behaving as if it wants to take the place of management.") When such a proposition is in danger of being articulated, a member of the group holding a contrary minority position—often in denial of the emerging proposition—speaks to that individual position, warding off the general proposition. ("I couldn't care less about management. I don't even know who they are.") This counterstatement is often made with strong authority, and nobody challenges it. This is because the others tacitly support the notion, even though it is unsupportable. You can see how the minority voice provides an alibi for the majority.

Tokenism and political correctness may serve the same purpose, confusing the issue, muddling the thinking. Having a black member of the group—or an isolated woman—defends the majority against the thought that it is still basically a white male group.

The giving and taking of authority for understanding the complexity of identity, thereby allowing for clarity of purpose, is what has to be subverted. Sabotage challenges consensus and majority politics. It is that part of human nature that says, I'll get you if it kills me.

Another example of sabotage is the holding of secrets, to be played with in private in destructive envy of relationships that are known about. The secret is about a possibly hopeful future. Sexual fantasies provide useful material for this kind of sabotage. In group relations conferences, external relationships—both working relationships and friendships—are often not spoken about, because of the fear of envious attack that any such disclosure would bring. But knowledge is power and secret knowledge is all the stronger, because it cannot be challenged.

The quality of the knowledge is dependent on the process of learning that got us there. Meltzer and Harris have usefully defined different kinds of learning, and I will give attention here to scavenging:

> [Learning by scavenging typifies] the envious part of the personality, which cannot ask for help nor accept it with gratitude. It tends to view all skill and knowledge as essentially secret and magical in its control of nature and people. It watches and

listens for items "thrown away", as it were, where no "please" or "thank you" need enter in, and therefore tends to feel triumphant over the stupidity of others for giving away the formula. [Meltzer & Harris, 1976, pp. 393–394]

Sabotage, being perverse, is destructive. This is because the sabotage lacks any aspiration to change the system; it wants simply to retain its parasitical space within the system. It is about survival, even if this means death.

Sabotage therefore defines the boundaries of our own imagination. This happens personally, in groups and in large complex organizations. Those who act unsocially, erratically, who use secret knowledge to subvert the task, are holding back and defending against aspirations to transform the future. Destabilization of the work is in the interest of no change.

We should not assume that subversion of the task of an organization is only done by a deviant sub-group of disempowered troublemakers—the equivalent from our school days of the back row throwing paper pellets when the teacher's back is turned. These are easily identified, although they are not easy to get rid of, given the constraints of employment legislation and political correctness.

If the subversion is to be really effective, it has to be with the collusion of a powerful (e.g., parental) authority within the system. I understand that, within the dynamics of a family, you sometimes need a bright child, who can recognize the truth, to enact a lie on behalf of the family. We may think of the gang in an organization working in a similar way. At first it is necessary sufficiently to recognize the truth in order to subvert it in the interests of a narcissistic authority that cannot distinguish the desire from the deed itself.

The gang in the organization behaves as if the task is to maintain triumphant superiority. Authority is perverted into dominance, and leadership is given to and chosen by the most charismatic liar. Ideas of narcissistic or pathological organization in mental processes have become familiar through the work of psychoanalysts investigating the borderline personality. Herbert Rosenfeld (1971) describes how the destructive narcissism of patients appears highly organized, "as if one were dealing with a powerful gang dominated by a leader, who controls all the members of the gang to see that they support each other in making the criminal destructive work more effective and powerful" (p. 249).

John Steiner (1987) argues that a pathological organization in the mind "functions as a defence, not only against fragmentation and confusion, but also against the mental pain and anxiety of the depressive position. It acts as a borderline area between the two other positions, where the patient believes he can retreat if either paranoid or depressive anxieties become unbearable" (p. 328).

The analogy that the psychoanalysts are making with work organizations in thinking about mental processes is an important associative link to make because work organizations, in their turn, may also have, as it were, a borderline personality. They also live in an uneasy space between a depressive position of institutional integration, continuity, and dependency and a paranoid-schizoid mentality of win–lose competitiveness, offering total success or annihilating failure, boom and bust. The overt task is sustained only when this struggle between the two positions does not get out of hand.

The gang in the organization acts in a way that only has internal reference and so is subject to accusations of poor judgement when things start to go badly wrong. A mature organizational culture, with a valency more to the depressive position than the paranoid-schizoid, is in fact safer in its operation of the primary task, because it recognizes that there is both failure and success and will be able to cope with both.

The concept of primary task has itself an uncertain history. A problem has always been to relate the notion of a single overriding task with the confusing and seemingly conflicting multiple objectives of a complex organization. Even as a heuristic device, the concept may seem to be lacking in credibility for those struggling with the uncertainties of managing in a turbulent environment or, worse, offering a self-deluding escape route for those who want to simplify things in the interest of having a consistent vision. I argue that the elusiveness of the concept, when it is not reduced to the pragmatic need of an economic agency of any kind to be profitable, is part of its usefulness; the struggle to determine and agree a notion of task is integral to the psychoanalytically informed study of systems.

The primary task of a system was first defined as "the task which it is created to perform" (Rice, 1958) and then as "the task it must perform if it is to survive" (Rice, 1965). These are not the same thing, of course, and in contemporary organizations we have to bridge these two meanings by exploring primary task in an organization whose survival is a question not only of financial health but more fundamentally about how it has retained the capability to carry out its original mission.

Primary task has been important in the Tavistock tradition of action research and consultancy as a heuristic device, because it allows the researcher to clarify the input–conversion–export process of an open system (Miller & Rice, 1967). As such, primary task may be thought by some critics to be important to organizational consultants first, and their clients second. From the beginning it offered, for example, a way of distinguishing different clients with contradictory primary tasks (Sofer, 1961). It is an exploratory tool of the consultant– client relationship; it distinguishes the dominant operating activities of the enterprise and does not confuse them with maintenance or regulatory activities (Miller, 1976).

However, the concept of primary task has also been used in a temporary, even opportunistic way, similar to the identification of critical success factors in managing an organization through a crisis. If there is one primary task "at any given time", as many definitions of primary task have been careful to state, then we must allow the possibility that there could be another primary task at another time, and most references to primary task in recent years have described the consultant's aim to work with a client system to "redefine" or "change" its primary task (Obholzer & Roberts, 1994). So the task of an educational establishment might be thought to shift from education to recruitment. Or there may be no settled order of priorities of task in, for example, a teaching hospital. However, this confuses the primary with the immediate task, which may indeed change from moment to moment, as in the operating theatre of a hospital, but always in the context of why the operating theatre was financed, equipped, and staffed in the first place.

Temporary or partial definitions of primary task may also be adopted in a self-seeking way to emphasize the interests of one stakeholder above others. This does not do proper respect to the concept of task. For the concept to be useful in a way that goes beyond temporary expediency, it has to contain some essential quality that is resistant to organizational politics. In addition to the idea that there is a task that the enterprise has to do in order to survive, it may be necessary to link this with an idea of the core business of the enterprise—or the task it has to do if it is to continue to survive *as itself* and not be transformed into something quite different. Thus a hospital has to provide services for patients, as well as provide employment, maintain research programmes, act as a commissioner for small businesses, and so on. Nevertheless, if it does not primarily provide services for patients, it is no longer a hospital, doing the task it was created to perform.

This task that a system was created to perform—the original definition—cannot, I believe, change radically from moment to moment, but how the task is then carried out can, of course, be transformed. There has always been an ambivalence about the use of the concept: is it opportunistic or determined? However, as the environment within which a system has to survive is thought of as increasingly turbulent, even chaotic according to the theory of complexity now being applied to human systems (Kauffman, 1995; Stacey, 1996), it becomes important to emphasize the *immanent* quality of primary task. At the same time there is a continuing recognition among those drawing on psychological research, despite the somewhat manic pronouncements of organizational change agents, that there have to be predictable relationships in the everyday world of work (Marris, 1996).

In Tavistock Institute action research with hospital systems, the idea of primary task was in fact important and helpful in order to try to determine an order of priorities of a complex system (Dartington, Jones, & Miller, 1974). Furthermore, in a system with an ill-defined reparative task—for example, getting people better or managing them into a kind of social death (Miller & Gwynne, 1972)—the definition of task may be seen as a defence both against omnipotence and against an overwhelming sense of guilt (Dartington, 1979).

This emphasis on the primary task of an organization as referring to essential activity that it has to undertake in order to survive as itself is helpfully provocative, in a context where it may seem to those working in organizations that anything goes, through re-engineering and similar attempts at dis-continuity, mergers, reconfigurations, down-sizing, the absurdist world of performance indicators and all the spurious collection of data that follows from that, and the apparent domination by command and control management. The NHS in the United Kingdom has experienced the repackaging of services in trusts—health services run as businesses (Pollock, 2004)—where they experience radical changes of organizational culture (Bruggen, 1997), with the introduction of purchaser–provider relationships to create a quasi-market in what had previously been cohesive bureaucratic systems of health and social care in the public services (James, 1994).

Menzies' paper on defences against anxiety is much quoted, and the phenomena she described in the nursing services in a London teaching hospital are with us still as strongly as ever in nursing and other professions (Menzies Lyth, 1960). Menzies would say, no therapy without research—no research without therapy. The essential characteristic of this approach is that it is collaborative. It means working alongside people in identifying issues that they find difficult and painful. And it has the potential to support and encourage the necessary autonomy of the effective worker and to counter the effects of an unexamined culture of dependency.

We manage ourselves in order to defend ourselves against anxiety, the underlying fear of annihilation, what Bion called "nameless dread", which from birth is part of the human condition (Bion, 1962). Otherwise we would not be able to function effectively and creatively. Menzies described in more detail the anxiety that nurses may experience through their intimate contact with the vulnerability, both physical and mental, of others. We are uneasily open to this anxiety every time we are in a new and strange situation. This is as true at work as in any other aspects of our lives. This is why it is important that we are clear about our roles and responsibilities and that we have clear procedures, training, supervision, and supportive management. However, even if we have all of this in place, it may not be enough.

Menzies showed that responsibility for intimate care of sick and dying patients resonated painfully with the nurse's unconscious anxieties, which made the nurse's individual defences precarious; in addition, various mechanisms in the social systems of the hospital could be seen as providing supplementary shared defences against these anxieties.

I would emphasize here that defences against anxiety are not bad in themselves: social defences are necessary to the everyday fraught business of living. The question is, are the defensive behaviours that we observe in ourselves and others functional, or at times dysfunctional, not only in carrying out the work—the overt task—but in doing the essential undercover work of helping us to feel that we can achieve psychic survival in the business of living?

Menzies describes how social defences in nursing—she observed the misdirection of responsibility up and down the system—may be dysfunctional, as

> nurses are deprived of positive satisfactions potentially existent in the profession, for example the satisfaction and reassurance that comes from confidence in nursing skill. Satisfaction is also reduced by the attempt to evade anxiety by splitting up the nurse–patient relationship and converting patients who need nursing into tasks that must be performed. . . . Success and satisfaction are dissipated in much the same way as the anxiety. . . . The poignancy of the situation is increased by the expressed aims of nursing at this time—to nurse the whole patient as a person. The nurse is instructed to do that, it is usually what she wants to do, but the functioning of the nursing service makes it impossible. [Menzies Lyth, 1960, p. 70]

Bion described man as a group animal, whether we like it or not—very often not. The basic assumptions underlying group life mean that we are never altogether removed from what may at times seem to be non-rational and dysfunctional behaviour. We are looking, therefore, to bring together the psychoanalytic theory of infant and adult development, and of group process, with an understanding of systems having a necessary relationship with their environment, and then of systems as having defensive qualities against the anxiety in the individual and the group. This way of thinking is further informed by the psychoanalytic contribution to understanding the relationship of the action research consultant to the organization she or he is working with. In particular, there is consideration of the transference and countertransference phenomena discovered in the analytic dyad. Feelings aroused in the patient and also, in response, in the analyst may offer clues to the nature of other relationships in the patient's life, including those earliest relationships that inform all that follows. Feelings aroused in the organizational consultant may also provide significant data about underlying processes in the client system. This is why a personal analysis has been considered to be an important part of the training of a consultant in this tradition. As with the analyst, the consultant has to provide a containing or holding environment that is safe enough in which to work with the anxieties and anger projected from the client system onto the consultant. I did not realize that this way of working was so unusual at the time, and it is only later in the research literature that the use of countertransference as a tool for research has been properly described (Jervis, 2009). Psychoanalytic observational methods, developed at the Tavistock Clinic first in relation to small children and their caregivers, together with the Tavistock methodology of work discussion groups (Rustin & Bradley, 2008), have been applied with success to older people in care settings (Davenhill, Balfour, & Rustin, 2007). In the same way, the concept of action research has come under increasing scrutiny and has been justified in the context of health and social care, where conventional research findings may be found to be of limited value to those working in practice (Meyer, Ashburner, & Holman, 2006).

Reflecting on my experience of this role, and my learning from successive engagements with systems of care, I have seen where there has been a wish both for unacknowledged dependency needs to be met—in the providers as well as the users of services—and an unacknowledged hatred of that dependency. This has led to the central hypothesis explored in this book: that health and social care systems have to manage the incompatible contradictions of human service organizations, working with heroic and stoical responses to the human condition.

CHAPTER THREE

Self and identity:
defences against vulnerability

The body does not belong to you, it is only cunningly
constructed clay.

Epictetus

It is in the context of an exaggerated sense of our own independent worth that mundane arguments about who pays for health
and social care have to be justified. A social system is devised
around a need, a need that is common enough to justify a pooling
of resources, a social as well as an individual response. So we have
crèches and schools, hostels and hospitals, asylums and a thousand
other projects that require capital expenditure, disinterested governance, and a respect for the vulnerability in others that we seek
to deny in ourselves.

We are all vulnerable, one way or another. Sometimes we pretend to be more vulnerable than we are, but mostly we deny it. We
are vulnerable most obviously to external forces over which we
have little or no control. Viruses, being no respecter of boundaries,
present a problem to our presumed omnipotence. Governments
take on responsibility for the management of epidemics, while

advertisements for common-cold remedies exhort us to indulge our omnipotence and act in denial of illness, able to make presentations, deliver reports. and win contracts as if nothing had happened to disturb the 100% efficiency of the bodily systems that we claim as our own. In contrast, a genetic predisposition to illness and decrepitude is difficult to explain away. If we live by the assumption that it is our body, it follows that any presumed defect or fault in that body is our fault. We blame ourselves, and, out of sympathy, society blames us too.

Jackie Kennedy Onassis was puzzled that she had cancer, when she had looked after her body so well. The issue of how much we have any control over the vulnerabilities of our lives is crucial to our moral and social understanding of the individual and the group. The contemporary perspective on the self as an autonomous tyrant in a land of opportunity means that, in our self-in-the-mind, we do not take prisoners but seek to do away with whatever gets in our way.

The phrase "self-made man" is given literal meaning by celebrity entrepreneurs, who promote their personalities as strongly as their products or services. Self-help manuals often seem to draw on principles of universal philosophy and new-age holistic meaning, but they are quickly subverted to the personal gain of the one-minute manager. The underlying principle is that you are on your own in what you achieve, and, to the extent that you are dependent on others, you seek in your mind to use them too.

This is also a new age of servants. There is a world of difference between the traditional working-class community-based perception of "going to the doctor" and the more affluent individualistic notion of "seeing my doctor"—and increasingly "my therapist", as well as "my accountant/financial adviser". In everyday life, we have as many servants now as the rich man in his castle. Executive coaches at work and life coaches at home give that individual attention that you need to confirm your position at the centre of the world. They act as personal valets, doing the job of Jeeves, helping to maintain the illusion that you have done it all by yourself. But we are not truly aristocrats who understand the responsibilities of privilege, and, unlike Bertie Wooster, we would like to deny our interdependence with these servants. If we think we own them, then it is as if we owe then nothing. So we set up systems of living that are potentially non-viable, a consumer society that is expected in some way to be independent of external factors in a global market.

Very few people can really be said to create wealth on their own. Even the solitary artist working in his studio, a Picasso, needed a flourishing art market and the assured wealth of others to give economic value to his work. This cult of the self may be examined for its unquestioned assumptions, as personal wealth is justified at the expense of an understanding of social capital. In what sense does a city trader earn his million-pound bonus? In what sense does a Russian entrepreneur own a fortune generated from the oil-rich frozen wastes of Siberia and invested in a football club, which is then able to afford contracts with millionaire footballers, who no doubt also believe that they are worth what their agents negotiate for them? Such earning and ownership is accepted because this process is not different in principle from the sense that we all have that our money, whether it comes as wages or share options or by inheritance, is evidence of our worth and is ours to do with as we like.

In a global economy that works through the interdependence of systems, made possible by technology, we continue to work on the assumption that we are the makers of our own wealth. If we have little wealth, then it follows that we are of little worth. A lot of wealth and we are people of importance, of influence, of judgement and taste that others would do well to follow. As Homer Simpson said, "How come pop stars have an opinion on everything?"

This idea of the independent self is in part cultural, a product of Western individualism. Partly also, I suggest, it comes from our innate human nature and is hard-wired into the structuring of our consciousness. Man is a social animal, but we separate ourselves from other animals by our individual consciousness, and this has been described both vividly and usefully in psychoanalytic thinking about how we perceive the world we are in. We use our first few months of life to learn our limits, exploring our fingers and toes and putting everything we can in our mouths, finding all the love and reassurance we need in the breast, the mother, the other who tolerates and rewards our omnipotent fantasy, and at the same time experiencing the terrible anxiety, the nameless dread brought on by the temporary absence of that containing other. So we begin to build an inner world that relates to but not equates with an external world of good and bad objects, that seem to make for delight and frustration, for love and for envy and hate. And then it is a task for the rest of our lives to reconcile these inner and outer worlds.

It is in our nature to make this separation of what is I and not-I, what belongs and what does not, and, like the babies we were in our cots, to hold close what is at that moment pleasurable and loveable and to throw out what is to be despised, destroyed, the hated objects to which we have ascribed such awesome power that we are fearful of their revenge.

This is the Western idea of self, on which we then want to put a good face. The cultural emphasis on self and identity, the basis of a consumer society, acts as a defence against our awareness of our vulnerability, and the negotiations that we make all the time to confirm our sense of self are crucial to our sense of worth. I experience myself as having an identity, and others confirm that in their relations with me. We get occasional hints of this. When I bought a four-wheel-drive car, I found that several friends expressed some surprise. They did not think it was my sort of car, obviously. But if you upset your friends' perceptions too much, they will worry about you. They will question your judgement and, at the extreme, will question your sanity. When I am underperforming, I say I am not myself today. Old friends say, he is not the man he was. I could say of my wife with Alzheimer's that she was not the woman I married. When we are not confident in these negotiations, we are vulnerable.

We believe strongly, then, in this continuity of identity and take note of any deviations. There was a time, which peaked with Harold Wilson, I think, when politicians obsessively declared the consistency of their view on every matter of policy. This assumption of consistency is maintained despite the fact that what we may need in reality are politicians who are capable of changing their minds. "Changing their minds"—that is the clue. To have a new thought is to change your mind? It is as if you become a different person. No wonder the psychoanalyst Bion said that we have a hatred of thinking.

It is not quite the same now. Extremes of relativism and social constructionism—where in fantasy you can be whatever you choose—are sometimes explained in the language of post-modernism and are linked to ways that society has become ac-culturated to what we may recognize as adolescent behaviour. In this "adolescentiation" of society, we now have the phenomenon of the makeover, where it seems that it is possible shamelessly to construct a new image of oneself. Children look older, older people look younger. And politicians now are always having to come up with new and younger policies, like adolescents who restlessly have to be uniquely different while slavishly following the conventions of their social group.

The characteristics of adolescence have to do with transition and transformation. The only makeover that used to matter was puberty, when the body changed from that of a child to that of a women or man. This process does not take long, a few months at most, but the process of adolescence has now stretched to extend from mid-latency, as children dress and act like their fantasies of adults, into adulthood and is continuing to expand into middle age. Adolescence is a state of mind characterized by desperate but temporary attachments, fierce competitiveness, and a preoccupa-tion with status. It is crucially self-absorbed, confusing high ideals and selfish acts. Its morality is built on ideas of fairness and the ambition to get more and more in order to get one's fair share. What was a temporary phenomenon while the hormones kicked in is in danger of becoming a continuing and long-drawn-out narcis-sistic love affair.

What this process threatens are some of the more materially irrelevant ethical issues: loyalty when it conflicts with self-interest, remorse when caught out trying to take advantage of an opportu-nity—what in public life may be insider dealing, selling favours, or other contemporary forms of fiscal and moral corruption and may also be corrupting of familial and community relationships of mutual trust.

A supposed maturity is then relocated somewhat later in life, when all the deals have been done. It is the state of mind of those who are taking, have taken, or would like to take retirement, to-gether with a certain detachment from adolescent urgency. We may think that there is a maturational transition in adult life, which may be associated briefly with a "mid-life crisis" (!), and then retirement succeeds adolescence as a state of mind, when we re-order priorities according to a different rhythm, valuing stability over status, and a wished-for predictability over the instant gratification of our desires. What looks like a nostalgia for a past that never really happened may be understood also as a recollection of latency, before the adolescent urge kicked in.

Of course, this is not the same as actual retirement—though it can be experienced as hanging on for that desired state, "just a few years to go" . Some people do not retire at all, and we may note that they are usually unchallengeable in their status, at the top of their chosen professions, a religious leader or the president of a one-party state, or anyone else with unquestionable authority (often in quite modest family businesses, for example). For many people, however, there is a de facto if unofficial retirement on grounds of ill health. We—or others—may feel that we just can't hack it any more. According to a mechanistic view, we are too run down to work properly, like a broken toy. At a societal level, an official retirement age has been a way of making sure that there is enough food (in every sense) for everybody, of clearing away the plates and making a space for the next meal.

Those of working age, and still employed while in this proto-retirement condition that I have described, may be looking forward to retirement, "hanging on", as they say: they express privately their increasing irritation and concern about the idiocies of organizational life. They worry about this. It is a bit like memory loss—forgetting the occasional name makes one anxious about impending dementia, but this is normal and not pathological. So they may be taking a mature and reflective view of a world run on principles of adolescent mayhem—where points mean prizes, short-termism is seen to be very clever and astute, and doing well means being obsessive about things that are not in the end very important. But they worry that instead they are becoming grumpy old men and women. The danger is that the negotiations about identity are beginning to break down.

We are all the time in dyadic relationships. One-to-one is often the preferred default position for resolving issues in private life, and then in therapy, in supervision, in coaching at work. But in the politics of identity we not only have to do a deal with the other:

there has to be a third party to the agreement. So we have to remember that the pair has always the potential also to be delusional. We have to keep in mind a third party to the relationship, the one that helps to keep us sane. This is what gives some context to the relationship of the pair and provides a wider reference, which offers a degree of safety against delusional thinking. This "third position" may be nothing more than an important attitude of mind; or it may be a role that is being taken by a mentor or advocate. This, however, is also the role of the regulator or the evaluator, and in the public sector now there is a whole industry of audit, so that the third position would seem at times to be crowding out the original pair. The sense of threat that is experienced in the dyad is understandable when there is an underlying wish there for an inward-looking self-idealizing closed system of mutual dependence. It has required a shift of thinking to acknowledge that "value for money" accountability (pioneered by medical insurance in the United States and developed by successive auditing authorities for health and social care in the United Kingdom) provides a necessary and healthy reference point.

However, this means that it is still important to investigate the authority of the individual in the system, and how one manages oneself in situations of stress and underlying anxiety, which is inevitably present when there is a therapeutic task. In this context, the defence mechanisms identified in Menzies Lyth's 1960 paper, though specific to the situation she was describing, have been seen to have a more general relevance.

In many ways, things have improved, in nursing as in other areas. Psychological trauma is widely acknowledged, even when it is not understood, and few people these days are unaffected by an awareness that it is important—necessary, even, for one's mental health and personal and professional effectiveness—to recognize that we are influenced in ways that are not obvious or immediate by experiences that put us in touch with primitive anxieties—for example, to do with death. Post-trauma counselling has moved from the periphery to the mainstream in the thirty years from Aberfan to Dunblane. At the same time Caroline Nicholson, a nurse, has researched how frail older people, having a need for intimacy, connection, and relationship, are "asked to hold and tolerate society's fear and sequestration of ageing, dependency and death" (Nicholson, 2009). Continuing care is not well resourced. Both staff and premises can look the worse for wear, a recognition of the lack of priority given to this area of nursing. Another nurse researcher, Cheryl Holman, has given a psychological explanation of the lack of planning and allocation of resources to such hospital wards, "as hostile projections connected to profound dependence, the limits of therapeutic endeavours and the fear and dread of emptiness and non-existence. . . . People outside the ward felt safe from the deep psychological disturbance they had projected into it" (Holman, 2006, p. 309).

The complex social defences that structure our relationships in order to cope with a stressful world are as important as ever—and the observation that we need such defences is not in doubt. The question is how to ensure that they are functional, both for one's own health—so that we do not become altogether cut off from what we are feeling—and also for our work so that we do not become insensitive to the needs of others, as happens when there is bullying at work.

Organizational life has changed in ways that are relevant to this question of our social defences. The world of work has changed over recent years and not always in the ways that were predicted. Computerization has led not to the realization of a zen dream of the paperless office but to an adolescent fantasy of instant gratification and an explosion of repetitive, useless, and misleading bits of information. A small example: a university professor—someone who is paid by the state to think—was puzzled by the demand that she record what she was doing every six minutes. The information she invented, out of a mix of puzzlement and mischievousness, is then given the status of fact, joining a vast number of other statistical viruses in the system. In such small ways we continue to infantilize those on whom we rely for adult judgement and wisdom. Infantilization of this nature is a dysfunctional defence against the complexity of organizational life.

The splitting up of the nurse–patient relationship, the detachment and denial of feelings that Menzies Lyth described, have evident echoes in those elements of macho-management that have become acceptable since the NHS reforms. Institutions with a therapeutic task used to be badly managed, in the sense that the social system and its management was over-influenced by professional—clinical or therapeutic—values. Thus the institution may become too permissive, too non-directive, and lacking in firmness and boundary control. This is still possible. But such autonomous states of self-indulgence are in stark contrast to the managerial culture of recent times, which is obsessed with performance. Performance anxiety may itself be a cause of impotence. But we now see the managerial stud, the business athlete, who is expected to perform with the minimum of foreplay and only token acknowledgement of the need for a meaningful relationship. Ritual task performance and an emphasis on checks and counter-checks have been further reinforced with a new emphasis on—and a new interpretation of—quality assurance, clinical audit, standards, and targets.

The effects of the collusive social redistribution of responsibility—those lower in the hierarchy being expected to be irresponsible if they are not watched, those higher being credited with exaggerated responsibility through a process of delegation upwards—have been experienced in the health services and elsewhere and may be observed concretely with the greatly increased differentiation of pay between senior managers and the humble or humbled workers.

We now have to live with much greater uncertainties of identity, as a life-time career and commitment become anachronistic, both in public and in private life. The question of personal development is interesting in this context. A stake in the responsibility for developing the workforce has shifted from employing institutions to become much more the responsibility of the individual. In a portfolio career you use your redundancy money and periods of unemployment to invest in your own development. In the short-term logic of the market, the employer—or purchaser—buys skills but does not develop them.

Consider our attitudes to nursing, as the traditional exemplar of the caring relationship. We may have to rethink the nurse–patient relationship as that of employee and consumer. This puts a very different emphasis on the question of accountability. As patients have, with some justification, become increasingly impatient of the services they are offered, we are exploring wider terms of reference within which to manage the relationship—for example, by giving attention to patients and service users as stakeholders. This has been the most significant contribution of the voluntary or not-for-profit sector to the development of human service organizations.

Governance should provide a reflective space for an organization to think. It does not always work out like that, of course, and there may be political obfuscation in the formal distribution of authority—think, for example, of the opportunistic distinctions between policy and operational matters that can be made by those holding political office who intervene when they need to be seen to act. However, one aspect of accountability that voluntary sector organizations have understood and have then helped the public sector to recognize has been accountability to stakeholders. The organizational chart for a drugs and alcohol agency, a flourishing provider in the current NHS market, has at the top, as you expect, its board of trustees, to whom the director reports, and so on. But above the board are placed the various stakeholders—the law, Charity Commissioners, Companies House, service users, purchasers, funders, commissioners, media, the public—to which the board is itself accountable. This wider accountability becomes part of the management-in-the-mind of those exercising authority on the ground.

Voluntary sector managers do not have for their protection the convenient fiction that anything and everything can be justified finally by reference to the interests of shareholders. Instead, they need to countenance the more complex possibility that the organization meets the needs of different stakeholders, whose interests are often in conflict with each other. These stakeholders include funders and donors, trustees, volunteers, staff, and beneficiaries. These different interests get tested in different relationships, and any one of these relationships may be thought of as subversive to the primary task of the organization

This complexity upsets command-and-control assumptions of good management. Although there is talk of empowerment and diversity, there are competing agendas for action. Formally the trustees hold the dominant vision—this accords with Trust law, which primarily serves the interests of the benefactor. But the authority of the trustees is not always sufficient or self-evident. With contracts and service agreements, government centrally and locally want to see value for money. They may not know how to look for it—but that is another matter. The institutional or formal authority of stakeholders is complemented by the personal autonomy and authority exercised by individuals, staff, volunteers, and users of services acting as if they hold shares in the organization. The phrase "publicly quoted" takes on a new meaning: stakeholders think they can say what they like about the organization—and expect to be heard.

Voluntary organizations survive, if they do, against a barrage of criticism and support from this Greek chorus. It is a certain kind of accountability, though different from that promoted in an audit culture. It is not accountability with sanctions, or being required to explain one's actions: it is more positive in intent, a responsive accountability. In theory this may be the weakest kind of accountability, but, if we get it right, it may be the most effective in achieving good management (Leat, 1988).

In reality, of course, voluntary organizations subvert this kind of accountability, because the people in them internalize a more difficult to define authority—what we might call accountability to the task or the mission of the organization. To do this successfully, the voluntary agency needs to have ways of maintaining its integrity of purpose against the threats of individual ambition, whether manifested as professional management or as unprofessional maladministration. There has to be an instinctive awareness of the secrets of the organization, its internal assumptions and organizational culture, among those acting as container for the anger behind the mission.

Many organizations in the private sector are more comfortable with a post-dependency culture. Employee engagement has come into favour: employees are enabled to exercise authority based on knowledge and experience in relation to a project, as distinct from conventional management authority, based on rank. The irony is that this is a kind of "psychological ownership", very familiar in the past in the workforces of voluntary organizations. It has been largely discredited in the drive for a new but already out-dated corporatism in the public sector according to supposed private sector models of good management.

However, an organizational culture that threatens the individual sense of self-worth of those who work in it, undermining an identity that owns the activity, is not going to be compatible with the task of looking after the needs of others. It is the capacity to manage oneself in role (Lawrence, 1979), within an organizational structure that sustains this capacity, that makes it possible to engage fully with the dependency of others without losing personal authority.

CHAPTER FOUR

The question of dependency

Man is a dependent creature no matter how autonomous he becomes.

W. R. Bion

In what circumstances can we think of an appropriate dependency of one person on others? To understand further the dilemma facing us in the provision of care for vulnerable people in our society, we have to revisit the whole question of dependency. Dependency always implies a relationship. On the one hand, there is the potential to give support; on the other, there is the fear or hope, desire for, or even expectation of that support.

An apparently neutral concept of dependency is nevertheless surrounded and coloured by ethical debate, psychological theory, and political philosophy, so that it may seem to emerge as not neutral at all: dependency bad—independence good. For example, dependency may be linked with a patriarchal model of family and other relations, where feelings of impotence are associated with a fear of and dependency on authority. It is helpful, therefore, in thinking about the meaning of dependency in human relationships, to make the distinction between primitive and mature dependency.

In the Tavistock group relations work, there has been much experiential study of dependency in human relations. Wesley Carr, following the example of a fellow theologian, Bruce Reed of the Grubb Institute, has tried to make an important distinction in his use of language:

> Dependence and dependency are obviously connected. But it is important to distinguish them, and particularly to show which is being referred to when the adjective "dependent" is employed. If it refers to an unconscious surrender of authority, then it can be addressed through interpretation and a shift from dependency to dependence and some sort of autonomy may be made. If, however, it describes a manifestation of appropriate dependence, then it is itself an exercise of authority. [Carr, 2001, pp. 5152]

While the distinction is useful in recovering a sense of authority for those in need of physical and psychological care, I would observe that this appropriate "dependence"—for example, in older people—often gets a response as if it is in fact "dependency", an abnegation of authority. There is, I would argue, an underlying fear of dependency, and this fear does not make a nice distinction between different ways of thinking about dependency.

In its primitive sense, dependency derives from a frightening and frightened state of mind, where the immature organism looks desperately in its environment for a reliable object to save it from unimaginable danger. This is true, say, of the crying infant, who then receives comfort and reassurance as well as food from the mother's breast. Later there is a process of weaning, where the child learns to tolerate a degree of independence.

However, the process of weaning is rarely, if ever, complete. We may observe in ourselves, as individuals and as members of social groups in different contexts, a tendency at times to put aside our own competences to deal with a situation and invest all competence in others. In this dependent state, where we are looking for our own gratification rather than doing what has to be done, it is difficult to be creative or productive. Anyone who has been in a meeting that seems to go on forever and is unable to make any decisions has experienced this phenomenon in everyday life. There is, moreover, a tendency in an unrealistic and often unconscious way to invest authority in a leader who will take away our fears and gratify our wishes.

Dependency in this sense has therefore been seen as pathological and destructive, and social institutions that are thought to encourage such dependency have themselves come under attack. Critiques of traditional institutional care have demonstrated that a system that only allows for the meeting of dependency needs—perhaps the need for help with dressing, eating, toileting of a person with disabilities—denies the capacity of the individual to take an independent decision-making role in relation to these dependency needs and all other activities. Care of elderly people is also complicated by the challenge to carers of all kinds to respond appropriately to dependency needs without infantilization.

It is important, therefore, also to have sense of what might be described as a mature or healthy dependency or "dependence". Without such a concept, a dismissive rejection of dependency in general terms as weak or pathological may be thought to lead to rampant individualism and a narcissistic egocentric view of the world. A mature dependency, in contrast, starts from a socio-centric perspective, where "No Man is an Island, entire of itself." Dependency in this sense is a very necessary recognition of the limitations of our own fantasies of omnipotence. It also avoids the perils of counter-dependence, a denial of dependency needs, a frustrated kicking against the constraints of reality that gets in the way of independent thought and action.

Mature relationships are grounded in the individual's developing capacity for attachment (originating in the bond between parent and child), trust, reliance on others, as well as self-reliance. John Bowlby, the psychiatrist and psychoanalyst associated with attachment theory, preferred these terms to that of dependence and independence, which look as if they are mutually exclusive (Bowlby, 1971).

The recognition of dependency, even if it is not overtly acknowledged, is essential to evolving processes of social behaviour, including the division of labour and the establishment of trading relationships. It is through the tolerance of mutually dependent relationships that social structures are formed and maintained. An example of mutual dependency would be the institution of marriage—for richer, for poorer, in sickness and in health. A mature dependency is not, then, about the simple gratification of needs, passively demanded of an often absent leader. It is an interactive process, requiring both thought and action, where there is a recognition of difference and a use of difference to achieve mutually agreed ends. An aspect of dependency is therefore a capacity for followership, for responding to the leadership being offered in a purposeful way.

Having made this distinction between primitive dependency and mature dependency, we have to acknowledge that the distinction is not so clear-cut as we work it out in everyday social interaction. This may be seen in a helping relationship, where a certain amount of regression to an infantile state of dependency is to be expected. In fact, it is arguable that the development of any relationship of trust requires the giving up of a certain amount of personal autonomy. This is why trust, as developed in a dependent relationship, is always open to the possibility of abuse.

It follows that an appropriate dependency puts a particular onus of responsibility on the person in a leadership role. The leader, receiving projections of omnipotence from others experiencing a certain regression, is therefore in a powerful position. This does not mean that the leader should summarily reject the dependency of others. That is likely to leave them confused and angry, and at a loss to know what to do. However, mature leaders may be working over a period of time to make themselves redundant in that role.

An example of that approach can be seen in certain kinds of consultancy relationship. The collected papers of Eric Miller have the overall title, *From Dependency to Autonomy*: "The intervention will be successful if clients have transformed the dependence on me into fuller exercise of their own authority and competence" (Miller, 1993a, p. xviii). Dependency is therefore not a chronic but a transitional state, evident at the beginning and end of life, and a necessary element in the management of transitions throughout life, where the individual is temporarily dislocated from the certainties of previous experience and thus more than usually reliant on the experience of others.

This is an argument for the recognition and respect for an appropriate dependency—in particular, in relation to services for people who are vulnerable in our society. It is surprisingly difficult to be neutral about this, to accept that dependency is a fact of life, from our first breath to our last. No one is going to speak up for an immature dependency, where we put aside our own competences in order to look for gratification of our needs in the competences of others. This is recognized to be pathological, so that a welfare state is described in derogatory terms as a nanny state, maintaining people in an infantile lack of autonomy rather than encouraging an appropriate reliance on one's own capacities to cope. The "personalization" of services is intended to allow for such self-reliance.

Andrew Cooper, Professor of Social Work at the Tavistock Clinic, has argued that there has been an important paradigm shift in the delivery of services. The shift is from an attention to "human emotional needs, human histories and the social relations that produce personal and social adversity" to a concern with barriers to opportunity (Cooper, 2007).

Opportunity here is linked to capacity and is evidenced by performance, ultimately by performance in the labour market. This includes the advantages to disabled users of social care services finding that funds are directly payable to them to purchase care in the local market of supply and opportunity. At the same time, the extension of governance has served to disperse responsibility for the provision of welfare across sectors, the old public sector, the private sector, and the independent or voluntary (not-for-profit) sector.

Cooper's argument derives from a study that he and Julian Lousada carried out on what they have called *Borderline Welfare* (Cooper & Lousada, 2005). They make a distinction between deep and shallow welfare: "The fear is that once we allow real contact with a deprived, dependent, helpless population, any services offered to them will become rapidly enslaved to their needs for all time, draining resources from other important projects, and depleting our autonomy and flexibility as a society and an economy" (p. 194) They conclude: "It is not dependency that is the problem, but fear and hatred of dependency" (p. 195).

My argument is, therefore, that we need to maintain the boundary conditions for an increased respect for dependency. The integration of health and social care systems, at both the micro- and macro-level, has always been an issue—but what I have realized, reflecting on my own work with hospitals and institutional care, is that we need primarily to understand why they are separated in the first place. And because the split is so deeply entrenched in the organizational culture of our welfare services, I am looking for a psychological underpinning for the rational arguments about efficiency and effectiveness and the political language about collaboration and partnership.

What is the real difference that is so difficult to integrate? In the care of older people, for example, social care is primarily about living with loss, compensating for ordinary activities that the ill or disabled person cannot do unaided any more—eat, go to the toilet, dress, sit, walk, or carry out any of these "activities of daily living" without assistance. Health care is more about fighting back, and although it includes many activities that are intentionally caring, these also include interventions that are new and special because the person is ill or disabled—and these interventions are often invasive, psychologically hurtful, and physically painful. There is an arrogance about foregrounding one at the expense of the other, but that is what we do.

And so we find that social care, as it is currently organized, is increasingly also about fight—short-term interventions to get you back on your feet—and if you really do have dependency needs, these will only be recognized at a late stage when a "panel", which does not publish its deliberations or decisions, determines that the individual is eligible, or not, for NHS continuing care. Currently, this happens at such a late stage that it may only access palliative care. In the meantime, health and social care agencies are both pursuing targets for short-term interventions, opening and closing cases and thus undermining any sense of continuity or overview of the person's long-term needs.

My hypothesis here is linked to psychoanalytic theory about the paranoid-schizoid and depressive positions in understanding the dynamics of our internal worlds in interpreting external reality. Services around vulnerable people are influenced by two states of mind, which are in a tension in relation to each other and difficult to synthesize. So we may observe two kinds of responses of the individual-in-society to our vulnerability to accident, illness, trauma, and debility. A split is enacted between the hopeful and the hopeless; between the active and the passive; between fight–flight and dependency; between resistance and acceptance; between an assumed omnipotence and a supposed impotence . . .

The first position may have some paranoid-schizoid characteristics. The citizen is approved for being aggressive, angry about what has gone wrong in one's life—"This is something that has been done to me." The appropriate stance is one of not accepting: the ills that one is suffering are not acceptable.

A friend died following a triple-bypass operation. Another friend, herself a manager in an NHS Trust, immediately phoned me to talk about the incompetence of the NHS. There is a splitting in society, which allows individuality and freedom of choice and at the same time a projection of responsibility on to others. What happens? The individual has a sense of grievance. This may be unacknowledged. This sense of grievance follows the experience of a psychological contract being broken. ("This could be a new baby in the family. I thought I was the one.") It is a state of mind that leads to acts that are anti-task or anti-institution. It involves a degree of self-perception—this may be conscious but split off. So feelings of guilt are pushed to the edge of consciousness. We become counter-dependent, fuelled by the sense of grievance.

The response is one of fighting back. After all, if you want something enough, you can have it. Failure, if it happens at all, is—or has to be—heroic. Vulnerability is for wimps.

The depressive position, which is also very much our experience in relation to health and social care, accepts more readily that stuff happens, good and bad, during our brief time in the world, and we have to learn to live with that. Hannah Segal, in her analysis of an elderly man, 73 years old, has described how he had come to see old age and death as a persecution and a punishment. In her work with him, he came to think of his approaching death

> as a repetition of weaning, but now, not so much as a retaliation and persecution, but as a reason for sorrow and mourning about the loss of something that he deeply appreciated and could not now enjoy: life. . . . But the mourning and sadness were not a clinical depression and seemed not to interfere with his enjoyment of life. . . . He might as well enjoy it and do his best with it while he could. [Segal, 1986, p. 179]

She reports that he lived another fulfilling eleven years.

How do health and social care services work with these two positions, as I have described—what we might call the heroic and the stoical? A lot of our lives are driven by the proposition that things can, indeed have, to get better. Government initiatives provide opportunities to get out of all kinds of a mess if you are enterprising enough—and if you are not enterprising yet, which is why you are in a mess, they will encourage you to become so. And indeed, these initiatives can and have made a very great difference to people's lives. Politicians reel off the statistics about the progress that has been made. But this opportunities agenda is not always successful all the time, and we all get caught out in the end.

Susan Sontag wrote about diseases as belonging to their time:

> The fantasies inspired by TB in the last century, by cancer now are responses to a disease thought to be intractable and capricious—that is, a disease not understood—in an era in which medicine's central premise is that all diseases can be cured. Such a disease is, by definition, mysterious. For as long as its cause was not understood and the ministrations of doctors remained so ineffective, TB was thought to be an insidious, implacable theft of a life. Now it is cancer's turn to be the disease that doesn't knock before it enters, cancer fills the role of an illness experienced as a ruthless, secret invasion—a role it will keep until, one day, its aetiology becomes as clear and its treatment as effective as those of TB have become. [Sontag, 1978, p. 5]

What Sontag described about cancer could be said now with equal force about dementia: intractable and capricious, mysterious, the insidious implacable theft of a life—a ruthless secret invasion. Clearly dementia has taken its place, in turn, as the disease that is a metaphor for a life destroyed by a malevolent twist of fate. How as a society we respond to this challenge is indicative of our capacity to think clearly about morbidity and death.

As a society we no longer believe in acts of god, the traditional let-out clause in insurance policies. Every attempt is being made to tie down any and every tragic event to human agency. Whatever goes wrong, someone is at fault. This, of course, is the basis for a litigious society. If a mother kills a child, a social worker is at fault—it is only a sophistication of the argument to say that there was a systemic failure. If there is not a straight line of argument to identify the perpetrator, a scapegoat will do. A disease without a known cause is provocative to our modern sensibilities in a way that has important repercussions in how we respond. The default position about any tragedy is that if another cannot be held to account, then the fault is one's own.

Put bluntly, as a society we punish people for having a disease that we do not understand and cannot cure, and for making us feel bad about them. At the same time that there is an awareness of the debility associated with increased life expectancy, there is an intensified media and political debate about assisted suicide, as an individualistic solution to an intractable problem.

As researchers at the Tavistock Institute working with issues of disability, we saw ourselves as trying to find a third position between the warehousing and horticultural positions identified in our study of institutional care. We wanted to retain a sense of the ambivalence of the wider society in relation to its disabled members. We deliberately focused this study on the distribution of attitudes around the disabled, to explore this ambivalence in action (Dartington, Miller, & Gwynne, 1981).

We had identified the humanitarian defence, that damage can be repaired, and the liberal defence, that there was nothing wrong with the person as such. Community care, we argued, was a non-acceptance of social death, though our experience of the community projects led us to see continuing aspects of institutional care alive and well even in the projects being initiated specifically in response to rejection of the negative aspects of that institutional care.

We were working with an open systems model, but not fully recognizing how the input–conversion–output model that was useful in thinking about operating systems was also relevant to the processing of group assumptions and individual attitudes in relation to disability and vulnerability. I later described this process in more detail, from the perspective of consulting to voluntary organizations:

> Inputs include an unfocused and often narcissistic altruism in individual donors, supporters and others, alongside more focused funding from grant-makers and purchasers of services; these resources are transformed by people, driven by enthusiasm and/or professional commitment and expertise,

and guided by policies that are both intuitive and determined, to achieve outputs, specific actions to meet a social need or moral end. [Dartington, 1998, p. 1490]

In the 1970s, the research team from the Tavistock Institute also worked with a geriatric hospital where the organizational problem we identified were the patients who neither died in the short term nor got better. I will describe some of the learning from that study in Part II. Those who neither die nor get better continue to represent the greatest challenge to health and social care systems. Thirty years later, researchers from the Tavistock Clinic found that senior managers in a social services department were calculating for above-average mortality figures during the winter months in order to meet government targets to do with delayed discharge.

The societal split between health and social care is evident even in the hospital ward. Older people (over age 65) are now occupying 60% and those with dementia are occupying up to 25% of hospital beds at any one time, and yet there are stories of unsupervised care assistants delivering meals to the end of the bed, without nursing oversight of the process (Age Concern, 2006). Lack of help with eating and drinking, when knowing an individual's routine would reduce anxiety and consequent challenging behaviour, is one of the biggest areas of concern, with two-thirds of family carers worried about failures of good practice. Older people unable to feed themselves, facing malnutrition and dehydration, overprescribed with antipsychotic drugs, as an Alzheimer's Society report (2009) has shown—these are not deliberate policies to achieve an accelerated level of mortality, but the outcome of policies that are fatally disrespectful of dependency. The problem will not go away, as an increasingly elderly population live to fight another day.

CHAPTER FIVE

The pursuit of common unhappiness

Much will be gained if we succeed in transforming your
hysterical misery into common unhappiness.

Sigmund Freud

My experience of the NHS at this time is as both provider
and customer of its services. In the tradition of open systems work at the Tavistock Institute, I have participated
in several interventions to make working in the NHS a less stressful experience than it sometimes seems to be for both managers
and clinicians. In one instance, with an NHS Trust, a workshop had
as its aim explicitly to understand and address issues of organizational stress, involving large-group work with participants drawn
from different hierarchical levels and functional areas within the
trust. I have often worked with staff groups in other trusts—for
example, a multidisciplinary group working with disturbed adolescents, with a therapeutic task that drew on both psychoanalytic
and systemic family therapy approaches. At the same time, as a
citizen I am also, of course, a patient or rather a customer of the

services that the NHS provides. The NHS is unique in this way: not only is it a major employer, but at the same time the whole of society uses its services. And as a citizen, like everyone in the United Kingdom, I have a stake in the NHS as a societal institution, and one that is more powerful in the public imagination, I would suggest, than any other.

An advanced industrial society has, as an aspect of its complexity, a technologically impressive and scientifically profound system of health care. In the United Kingdom this is identified with the state, and we call it a national health service. The impassioned arguments that continue in the United States whenever there are proposals to introduce a comprehensive heath care system in that society suggest that this relationship of the individual and the state touches on deeply held beliefs about autonomy and free will. Samuel Smiles, in his nineteenth-century treatise on self-help, stated: "No laws, however stringent, can make the idle industrious, the thriftless provident, or the drunken sober" (Smiles, 1859). The state is, however, heavily embroiled in our well-being in all sorts of ways, and, consistent with a mixed economy, the NHS works alongside and overlaps with private enterprise. In addition, as in any society, informal care is provided in the context of ordinary social relationships. Altogether there is an investment—both economic and humanitarian—commensurate with the resources of a society that is, relative to its own history and the rest of the contemporary world, wealthy. And yet the return on this investment seems to be profoundly unsatisfactory and insufficient, giving rise to a disappointment in the efficacy of its interventions, as recorded in the old bulging files of "heart-sink" patients in GP surgeries and now the job insecurity of chief executives of NHS Trusts. There is a banality about the human condition that fails to satisfy the political imagination. In the words attributed to Alfred Austin, a nineteenth-century political journalist and later poet laureate, about the then Prince of Wales:

> Across the wires the electric message came
> "He is no better, he is much the same."

It is possible to argue that this is a sick society and that health care resources have to run ahead of themselves in order to stay still. Or that the resources are wrongly directed, treating the symptoms and never the cause. Or that they are misappropriated, going to pay for GP contracts without the evidence of increased productivity. Medical practitioners used to have a high level of autonomy, retaining their status as independent practitioners in the newly formed NHS, and it has been a slow and expensive process to make them respectful of guidelines and targets. Such arguments challenge both people and systems, testing their benign intentions. But in making such arguments, I suggest we also have to examine the assumptions we make about health and illness before making judgements about the effectiveness of health care systems.

Health systems are inevitably subject to societal dynamics. A Chancellor of the Exchequer, with his eye on the big-spending Department of Health, described the NHS as "the closest thing the English have to a religion" (Lawson, 1992). OPUS identified the failed dependency of our major institutions. Safe institutional structures became unreliable, "no longer to be relied on as sources of employment and prosperity but they are also too fragile to cope with the force of our negative projections. These have to be taken back by the individual, whose props to identity are already undermined either by unemployment or uncertainty of employment, and reprojected on to 'society'" (Khaleelee & Miller, 1985, p. 380). One powerful symptom that supports this hypothesis has been the increase in violence that is directed against those who are there to help us, from firemen to nurses. I notice in the waiting area of my local hospital, next to the privatized cafe and newsagents (an improvement in efficiency on the WRVS tea bar, but a loss of atmosphere), there is a notice about assaults on staff. There is a solicitor's advertisement in Accident & Emergency, so you can get your wound sutured and think about your claim for damages at the same time. The Patient's Charter, like all good things, has unfortunate side-effects, I suggest, in a litigious culture, where perversely it is seen as therapeutic to harbour a grudge and take revenge.

In the 1990s, OPUS study days demonstrated how the individualism associated with the neo-liberal economics of the market has led to a shift from citizenship—where there is a trade-off between rights and responsibilities—to consumerism—where there is an actual trade in products and services, and the customer is said to have a choice, while services are outsourced, care staff become redundant, and product lines are discontinued—for example, NHS residential care for older people, now transferred to the independent sector. In many different circumstances, when the self-sufficiency of the individual is challenged, we expect a violent reaction: road rage is an example (Dartington, 2001).

Consumerism in the NHS, as in other areas, has led to a split between customer satisfaction and employee satisfaction. In the action research study of organizational stress in an NHS Trust, I heard little in favour of the Patient's Charter from hardworking and dedicated staff. Instead, they felt misunderstood and defensive, being made to take responsibility for a lack of resources that they could do nothing about.

The state has always been interested in the fitness of its fighting men—encouraging archery in the Middle Ages, seamanship in Tudor times, and shamed at the end of the great Victorian era that half the recruits for the Boer War were found to be medically unfit. In the next decade, national insurance was introduced, followed, after the First World War, by the establishment of the first Ministry of Health in a British government. The Labour Government elected after the Second World War introduced the National Health Service. William Beverage estimated the annual cost of the service at £170 million. It was even argued that good treatment would lead over time to a need for less medicine. After three years, the cost was £400 million. And in the present day, from 2003 to 2008, it doubled from £45 billion to £90 billion, with more than 1.3 million NHS employees.

Our societal expectations of the NHS are ever more complex. The challenge now in our age of anxiety has extended to the mental health of the working population, as one of the aims of the IAPT (Improving Access to Psychological Therapies) programme is "helping people stay employed and able to participate in the activities of daily living".

We may recognize the dependency we feel towards an institution that mediates between life and death, that defines happiness, that acts as a moral arbiter. But in a consumer society, the health service has another side. Rather than act as a container for our projections of omnipotence (alongside our ever-present fear of annihilation) on to the benign object, the health service may seem, perversely, to stimulate the consumer's omnipotent fantasies of self-sufficiency. Those who work there are not, then, the angels of our imagination but aggressors against our immortality. Menzies Lyth described the effects of the anxiety that is in all of us about survival. When we cannot cope with this in ourselves, we demand that our institutions cope on our behalf. The experience of the last twenty years has been that, in societal terms, we have had to grow up a little—to recognize that our institutions cannot provide that blanket reassurance. Every so often there is a panic attack: in recent times, both the banking crisis and the expectation of a flu pandemic have tested that maturity—can our institutions cope?

People with disabilities have suffered throughout history, and still, despite significant advances in recent years, they experience discrimination for both their real and their imagined deficits. Until recently adults with disabilities though of sound mind could be prevented from marrying because those managing resources did not think it appropriate to provide the necessary accommodation, an infringement of liberty that would be thought intolerable in relation to the most non-coping of the "able-bodied". To live one's life as a client of state-run services, at the mercy of others' judgements of one's own best interests, will not be done away with in the politics of personalization. We have seen a gradual shift of emphasis from the fatalism of a dependency on "God's will" to a dependence on the state, with the inevitable consequence of rationing of resources, where the quality of people's lives is assessed according to value-for-money criteria—for example, by the QALY (Quality-Adjusted Life Years) calculation used by NICE (the National Institute for Clinical Excellence).

The regulation of health care has become a preoccupation of government. The Audit Commission was set up by the Conservative Government in 1982 and the National Audit Office in 1983, with responsibilities for overseeing the economy, efficiency, and effectiveness of local and central government. This was part of a trend whereby inspectorates were created or enlarged for schools, universities, social services, prisons, and other public services. (It has been estimated that by the mid-1990s there were 135 different regulators overseeing the performance of the public sector in the United Kingdom, spending between them about £770 million a year or 0.3 per cent of total relevant government expenditure. This was double or even quadruple the level of public sector regulation that had existed in 1975. The Labour Government of 1997 continued the trend, creating new national regulatory agencies like NICE and the Commission for Health Improvement. It also introduced reform of professional self-regulation for doctors, nurses, and other clinical professionals and instituted a powerful new national regulator for private healthcare, the National Care Standards Commission (Walshe, 2003).

The chief executive of an NHS Trust has said that our health service might more accurately be described as a keep-death-at-bay service. "Hospitals are as much an embodiment of a social system that exists to defend society and its citizens against anxieties about death as are churches; from a psychic point of view, doctors occupy a similar niche to priests" (Obholzer, 1994, p. 171).

Clinicians who are also managers are often preoccupied with the working-out of the commissioner–provider relationship in the quasi-market of the NHS. Very accurately, in psychological terms, this has been called a purchaser–provider split. But the changes in the NHS go back to an earlier seminal moment, the introduction of general management on the recommendation in 1983 of Sir Roy Griffiths, a leader in the expansion of retail services. The importance of this is not simply that it means a single operational hierarchy to replace the previous tripartite arrangements, where individual clinicians had a dominant influence. There was an important shift of meaning, in the sense that we can now see management rather than clinical leadership as taking on the characteristics of a secular religion, a panacea, a blessing, promising wholeness, progress, worth, a challenge and a commitment. General management is a philosophy, a doctrine even, leading to a new order. Stephen Pattison and Rob Paton at the Open University have identified a number of parallels between evangelical Christianity and management theory and practice (Pattison & Paton, 1997). I will briefly extract some points from this comparison: Perfection (quality assurance, excellence) is to be sought by all members of the organization. Managers are known by their fruits: individual performance targets. Theories and statements about the organization must be clear, simple, and indisputable.

Because of their charismatic authority, managers are in a unique position to identify the vision towards which the organization should be working and to empower their followers to bring this vision to reality. The faith of the modern manager is a forward-looking optimism, which is defensive against the anxiety provoked by thinking about chaos.

One of the earlier manic gurus of this faith in management was Tom Peters (1989), and one of his commandments to guide his followers to organizational salvation was "Learn to love change". The alternative is death in an increasingly chaotic, competitive, and challenging environment.

In this context we may usefully look at the characteristics of the authority of the clinician and also that of the manager. Who in this context is the visionary, thriving on chaos, sticking with the negative capability that Keats ascribed to Shakespeare and Bion adopted as appropriate to the psychoanalyst? And who is the realist, the defender of tradition, structure, order?

Bion described the relationship between the mystic and the establishment. In his discussion of container and contained, he argues that the establishment has to find and provide a substitute for genius, for the mystic who may be both creative and destructive (Bion, 1970). But if management takes on the characteristics of a secular religion, we may wonder what happens if the establishment itself gets mystical. Who then is the mystic, and who is the establishment?

For myself in my role as patient, I might imagine that the authority of the clinician is individualistic, autonomous, an authority that derives from competence in relation to a task that is about life and death. In my fantasy, he or she is the sayer of true things, however uncomfortable.

The authority of the manager is, in contrast, systemic. I define the task of management as providing the necessary conditions in which people can get the job done. Among other things, this may include leading others into battle, reviewing performance and evaluating success, and also burying one's dead. It is an authority that requires some permanence and dependability, but the lack of job security of senior managers has become notorious in a culture of audit and moving targets. The NHS chief executive mentioned above had five changes of job in the twelve months before he took up that appointment in 2006.

There are occasions when I think that the roles may have become reversed, as management takes on the visionary role and the clinician struggles to provide for the dependent needs of those who are vulnerable to chaos and change—in their bodies, in their lives.

Before many of the changes in the NHS that now preoccupy us, I remember consulting to NHS systems and encouraging doctors and nurses to think that they were managers, and their hating us for this. I heard a psychiatrist contrast an NHS ethic where the quieter voices are heard—where there is cooperation and healthy development, where there is altruism—with a competitive market culture, where the survival of the fittest means that the meek will not inherit the earth after all. He referred to a previous clinical leader who had so antagonized the managers that they took retrospective revenge when the next cuts were to be implemented. Such a leader represents all our fantasized pasts, before the accountants inherited the earth—that golden age of infantile genius, when we could do the important work we believed in for no other reason than we believed it to be important.

This argument brings us not to determining nostalgically what was right or wrong about the good or bad old days but to the importance of mourning. In our OPUS consultancy work with an NHS Trust on organizational stress, we found that a workshop to explore some of these dynamics had been arranged, as it so happened, on the anniversary of the death of a long-serving nurse. This person had committed suicide, unable to face the changes that had been introduced—including the closure of the ward where he had worked for many years. The whole hospital was now facing closure, and the mental health trust would soon be working from forty different sites. The managers were enthusiastic about the changes—the improvement in the physical environment for patients and staff, the smaller units, the integration of inpatient and community services. But the changes were at the same time forcing a separation of work and other aspects of their lives on those who had worked in the hospital before it became the trust. The sports and social club was in decline long before it was closed. As organizational boundaries became more permeable and lateral relationships lacked the distinctive authorities attached to hierarchies, the hospital as an organization also was losing much of its institutional meaning, the "institution-in-the-mind that is formed out of the fantasies and projections of those who work in and around its functional operations" (Shapiro & Carr, 1991).

The managers had the vision, but others carried the sense of loss and the concern that the community out there would be a poor substitute for the community of the asylum, a secure place of refuge and shelter. It was only through interpretation of the dynamics of the hospital closure that managers recognized that it was necessary to allow for appropriate mourning in their management of change.

PART II

THE SURVIVAL OF THE UNFITTEST

CHAPTER SIX

The management challenge

That theme, of helping people to gain greater influence over
their environment, underlies virtually all my work...

Eric Miller

We may think that systems of care exist always to perform some social good. The prototype is the family, an
interaction of different generations within a gene pool
and an investment in its survival through succession. The family
is both a private arrangement, based hopefully on mutual love and
respect, and a public form of social engagement, in which society
at large also has an investment. This is recognized in very practical
ways, through tax breaks and benefits and in the provision of social
services working with family breakdown and abuse. So this is not
to idealize the family—violence and murder, sexual abuse, and
unthinking cruelty are also more likely to take place in the family
than in any other societal relationship. But the family, generally
speaking, is also thought to be good at looking after its own and is
genetically programmed to do so, providing opportunities for its
members to thrive and seeing to their needs.

Systems of care around vulnerable people are societally based—that is, they represent a public interest—and are supportive to or alternative to this prototypical family model of social being. They may seem to fit with a family model or develop very different kinds of organizational behaviour.

In all cases there is a tension about the meaning of care—what is thought of as good care—and this tension may be observed by considering what task is to be achieved in any context, what the appropriate response is to the need being expressed. Thinking about care is also always political: recognizing a need also immediately implies an acceptance that there is going to be a demand on resources.

Any crisis sets off a cycle of need. We can see this in ordinary family dynamics. A child complains of feeling ill. His mother makes an assessment, decides whether he is able to go to the school or not—does he need to be made comfortable and allowed to rest, or got back on his feet as soon as possible?—and makes this judgment in full awareness of the consequences: if he stays at home she will be late for work, but if he is ill he must be looked after. Assessment, intervention, convalescence may be over in a few seconds—in the time it takes for a cuddle—or, in a serious instance, may stretch over weeks or months or years. This everyday family dynamic is replicated on a much larger scale in the provision of public services.

The tension in care has to do with getting the response right for the seriousness of the crisis and locating where we are in what may be an iterative cycle of responses. Different systems of care attempt to locate themselves at different points of the cycle—for example, claiming to be the "end of the line" even when they are not—and they are always likely to be caught out by the every-changing needs that they are facing.

Within an ordinary family, or the wider community, it is not difficult to love a healthy child. The satisfactions and rewards that come from the relationship, from the intimate to the casual, are obvious enough. Complex psychological and ethical issues are also a part of ordinary experience, and a sick or disabled child may be loved even more fiercely. Myriad charities have been set up by mothers and fathers fighting the cause of their children. We do not need to look for evidence of the protective power of maternal love.

This protective love for the child is, at its core, instinctual—we are programmed to care for our young, as are most sentient beings. This love is expressed also by fathers, siblings, grandparents, and other family members, and by all kinds of surrogates.

What, then, about the care of older people? They are neither useful to the gene pool nor do they contribute much to the gross national product. Why are we caring for them? They may have residual economic power, having accumulated wealth to be passed on to a future generation through inheritance. They may have the detached wisdom of their years—like the old man in the films *The Severn Samurai* and *The Magnificent Seven*.[1] They may have retained creative strength in later life—we think of the example of writers, artists, musicians. But the question does not go away: while child-rearing or its equivalent is endemic in the sentient world, the care of the old is not, so why look after those who are not going to be able to return the favour, who have nothing left to give? And those living with dementia provide the severest test of our theories of altruism (Badcock, 1986).

The ambivalence in society about hospital care of the elderly is captured for me by the following experience. The Tavistock Institute action research study at Cowley Road Hospital in Oxford followed a series of harrowing reports and inquiries on care of the elderly: the Department of Health was worrying about the stress on nurses, and in Oxford a pioneering and charismatic geriatric physician was implementing radical proposals for what he called progressive patient care, so this seemed a good site in which to explore an open systems approach to the nursing experience of working with the elderly (Miller, 1993b). But the old people and their families whom we interviewed identified the hospital as the old workhouse and the last place they wanted to end up—and not even then if they could help it, with its workhouse associations of separation and social disgrace. Some years and several NHS reorganizations later I drove down the Cowley Road, and there were placards everywhere—Save Our Hospital—as the local people protested about the impending closure of the hospital and the loss of an important resource to the community.

This action research project followed the controversial study to do with physical disability, which had explored the concept of social death within institutions providing physical and psychological refuge through the "warehousing" of people ex-truded from the wider society and for whom, by and large, there was no going back. "In other words, the institutions import the socially dead and export the physically dead" (Miller & Gwynne, 1972, p. 161). If this was not to be a counsel of despair, it required an integration rather than a polarization of what the earlier study had identified as warehousing and horticultural models of care. Neither on its own was sufficient.

In the Cowley Road Hospital study, which I describe in more detail in the next chapter, some patients got better in a few days, and others died. They offered no problem to the system. But those who neither got better nor died were an institutional headache. We observed a process of integration and fragmentation, where a discrepancy emerged between what was the overt task of the staff working in the hospital system and what appears to happen to the patients at different stages of the treatment and care (Dartington, 1979). This discrepancy, which emerged on the first day of the patient's stay in the hospital, resulted from a splitting of percep-tions of what the hospital is supposed to be good at—providing specialized medical and nursing and other care—and what the community is perceived to be bad at—maintaining old people as functioning and valued members of society.

The tensions between the hospital and the community in this wide context were replicated systemically within the hospital be-tween the acute and the continuing care (then called "long-stay") wards, and in the tension between a medical leadership to do with intervention and a nursing response to do with giving comfort to those in distress.

At the same time that this study was taking place, a Tavistock Institute colleague David Towell was the social science adviser at Fulbourn Hospital near Cambridge, where he worked with the staff in designing and implementing innovative programmes to meet perceived deficiencies in the care being provided to patients (Towell & Harries, 1979). What made it possible for them to do this work? Miller described the necessary conditions as follows:

> By my definition every employee is a manager. . . . The notion that groups of staff have the capability and authority to take initiatives and that it is the task of managers of wider systems to provide the boundary conditions within which nurses and

other staff can perform their task more effectively seems, however, to be at odds with the culture of prescriptive superior–
subordinate relationships that prevails in the NHS generally.
[Miller, 1979, p. 190]

Since then, the NHS has experienced a succession of change initiatives. It seems a different age since we were saying to clinicians
that they were managers—before the introduction of general managers, and then of ever more insistent and emotionally detached
external systems of audit and control. We saw how the focus of
the dependency relations changed with the shifting balance from
institutional to community care. But the nature of the underlying
dependency in care relations has changed very little, as this serves
a function of keeping at bay the feelings of anger and aggression
that the work arouses (Dartington, Miller, & Gwynne, 1981).

Towell reported how one nurse at Fulbourn Hospital reported
that she was thinking about the ward when she was at home and
trying to think of other things to make it better. A couple of nurses
recognized for themselves that they found it difficult to make the
adjustment from the traditional rigid routine. And Towell and
Miller knew that it would not take much for the experiment to lose
impetus. Nevertheless, this is an example of what can be done if
there is recognition of a proper autonomy at the local level. And it
also says a lot for a methodology based on careful observation, in
conditions of sufficient trust and containment that allowed those
working in the system to attempt some integration of a warehousing approach to intractable problems with an interventionist
approach in reaction to the perceived passivity of a dependency-
based service.

At this point in the argument, the family and the state (representing the interests of the wider society) may be seen to have
recognizably divergent views. There is a view that families are
limited in their capacity for care, and that societal–state provision
has to take over. This may be described as the "reality" position.
(What is "realistic" is always a moving target. What we thought
to be the limits of what was realistic in the provision of care forty
years ago would be unacceptable today, certainly in disability
services. Conversely, what could helpfully be expected then for a
patient recovering from a stay in hospital—a period of recovery in
a convalescent home, for example—would not be realistic now.)

There may be negotiated agreements to manage such boundary expectations between formal and informal systems of care. This is the basis for providing day care, institutional care, hospital care— as alternatives to the family system of care—in response to the increasing dependency of old people (Burton, 2007). Supportive resources—home care—will also have been provided since 2003, according to a government-inspired framework of Fair Access to Care Services (FACS), which have in effect ensured that there are very few public services for those with "low" to "moderate" needs, compared to those assessed as having "substantial" and "critical" needs—which may mean, not until the family system is seen to have reached a stage of not coping or collapse.

But this rational linear model of the provision of care is not the whole story. Families may be rejecting of their frail elderly, but they also often experience reluctance, guilt, and regret that they "had no choice: mother had to go into a home". This is a dynamic that goes largely unexamined.

The societal–state response works largely from an assumption that publicly funded services are there to cope with the supposed rejection by the family. What goes unexamined is any critique of this scenario of rejection. The family system of care may in fact retain a stronger sense of the humanity of its elderly members, may want to look after them, to do more for them, than the societal–state perspective would acknowledge. This is the basis for the divergence that develops between the different systems.

The divergence is crucial to the delivery of services, for example, in the care of older people in hospital. I wrote at the time of the Oxford study:

> The way people come into hospital and the decision to make the hospital their refuge is such that the continuity of experience is often broken. The patient really has come, as it were, out of the void. Staff may even feel that it is necessary to keep a distance from what is outside to avoid a clash of values. But the services provided by the hospital for the elderly are better understood in the context of values in our society. The immediate family is expected to take care of its elderly members either by itself or with help from neighbouring kin. Contrary values however emphasize achievement and con-

spicuous consumption, with the implication that the possibility of becoming old, crippled or poor has to be put aside and denied. The elderly are expected to keep pace and are judged to be failing when they are not. Institutional care may be associated with the spectre of the workhouse or advocated positively as the best solution in the long run. While there has long been a trend to reinforce the advantages of family and community care, there are also demands, often in very painful and stressful circumstances, for institutions to take over the problems of the family by removing their infirm aged members. The geriatric hospital is only one of a number of systems of care working in a confusing and ambivalent world of contrary values, where the taking of responsibility for decisions made may be as important as the content of the decisions themselves. [Dartington, 1983, p. 93]

My earliest research, on the organization Task Force, included case studies on the relationships of young volunteers with isolated older people in inner London boroughs. The organization had been founded out of a belief in a kind of dutiful altruism: its founder Antony Steen, later an MP, described himself then as a "'middle-class boy made good', and believed that the greater one's social advantages the greater one's social responsibilities" (Dartington, 1971, p. 6). It was an organization of young people, thriving at a time of what may now seem naïve idealism about a "participant society". Would schools now so easily find space on their timetables for students to go unaccompanied to befriend and do practical jobs for elderly people living on their own? "The volunteers described here are not revolutionaries. They do not talk of social injustice but of the welcome they get every time they visit" (Dartington, 1971, p. 127). It would seem that they were acting as surrogate family, according to the principles of reciprocal altruism that is quite usual in that context.

What, then, about the needs of old people in hospital? In the study of geriatric hospital care as an open system, we saw clearly how implementation of what we may call a dynamic and interventionist approach, in contrast to a predominantly custodial approach, had demonstrated that a large number of patients who might otherwise have been bedfast in custodial institutions could be returned to the community after a fairly short stay in a geriatric hospital. The open systems approach inevitably focused attention on the interrelatedness of different systems.

> The notion of primary task ensures that there must be emphasis on one particular process. Thus the essential input of the hospital is seen as people needing treatment, and its output may be put broadly into three categories: those who have improved, those who have been referred for treatment elsewhere, and those who have died. In this way one may ascertain the primary task of the organization. In a hospital the task of giving treatment to patients must have priority. It is around this task that other tasks (the employment of staff of different experience and expertise, the training of staff, research, development of appropriate methods of treatment, and even the provision of social education in the highly emotive areas of sickness and health, life and death) may together make up a more comprehensive picture of what we mean by hospital. [Dartington, Jones, & Miller, 1974]

What we have seen in the development and delivery of services is an increasing division of labour at the same time as there is an awareness of the need for integration of services around the needs of the whole person. Why this division of labour? We understand the rationale of division of labour in manufacturing—first of all in pin-making factories, as observed by Adam Smith and celebrated today on the £20 note; later in motor cars, as exploited by Henry Ford. But in human services the rationale has surely to be different. We have a continuing development of specialisms—and, so it seems, the need to create the equivalent of the assembly line as the individual patient or client is assessed and reassessed according to all kinds of different criteria, for a multiplicity of needs.

But this image of the assembly line is not helpful—our experience as patients does not fit happily with this approach. For a social services client, negotiations might need to take place with up to twenty other organizational units, GPs, health visitors, home helps, hospital services, old age psychiatrists, residential home managers, physiotherapists, occupational therapists, day care centres, and so forth. There is no single overall organization to act as container to appreciate and reward collaboration (Dartington, 1986). Attempts to deal with the fragmentation in piecemeal fashion have led to a loose amalgamation of professions and functions—for example, in community mental health teams—where those working in the team, while holding on to their professional identity, at times feel deprived of identity and respect, the same sense of deprivation that they observe only too vividly in their clients.

The experience of losing role and therefore identity is key to our understanding of the concerns facing those working in a multidisciplinary context. They then become unconsciously allied with the older person who has lost a definitive role in society—a role where they know they could be useful to others, but a role that, at the same time, goes unrecognized and unvalued.

So we may see how the issues raised in a consultation with front-line workers about their clients are of the greatest importance for thinking about the overall management of services. The challenge for management is that it is not enough to integrate people—for example, in multidisciplinary teams—if you do not also integrate the systems in which they are expected to work. Yet the reality is that not even the computer systems could be made compatible.

There are, furthermore, two alternating perceptions of management at work, which are looking for an appropriate response to the conflictual definitions of task in the health and social care of vulnerable people. The perceptions alternate in the sense that it is possible to flip from one to the other in a moment and without notice. The first perception is of management as out of touch, arbitrary, and deeply problematic—perhaps like a dementing parent, out of touch with what you are having to struggle with. This management has to be mollified, or ignored, reluctantly loved and actively hated. The second perception is of management as a caring parent, doing her best in impossible circumstances, understanding of our difficulties, someone we do not want to put pressure on, but sometimes on whom we need to take out our frustration. This management is seen as exhausted, itself needing but not having recourse to respite care.

Closing the long-stay institutions in the 1970s did not do away with the dynamics of exclusion. The management challenge in this import–export business of health and social care has also now to provide for the dependency needs of staff in the context of a can-do management environment looking for short-term outcomes. Performance targets can be painful. As we have seen, it may be necessary that mortality in the elderly population reaches or exceeds the projections in last year's forecasts to meet targets on delayed discharge from hospital.

Managers, distanced but often in touch with their previous clinical identities, are very uncomfortable to find that they are thinking in this way. And yet the underlying realities of social death continue to affect the implementation of policy. In one local authority where I have been working in recent years, the managers are uneasily aware that there are very different responses in competing parts of the system to the imperatives to make economic cuts. Children's services were thought to be more able to hold firm against the financial pressure, while older peoples' services continued to make cuts, closing continuing-care wards. The public health agenda goes unheard in the clamour about cuts in acute services.

In the integration of health and social care, there has to be respect for difference. Otherwise a part of the reality is always going to be obscured. Incontinence has a primary meaning to a health worker of infection, while to a social worker it immediately means a loss of independence. Likewise, the concept of end-of-life care will have different meanings for health professionals and for social care professionals (Froggart & Payne, 2006). There is a lot of careful work to be done, giving space for thought at all levels in the organization, in the integration of services, and in new forms of integrated organizations.

What can we do to relieve the pressure that everyone experiences and to allow for the expression of caring and therapeutic skills? Reorganizations and reconfigurations often seem to drive professional groups into competition with each other, by forcing them into an intimacy for which they are not yet ready, rather than developing the cooperation that is necessary for survival and to keep the whole person in mind in providing services. Without time to build a necessary trust, individuals look to their own needs and cannot easily function together (Cooper & Dartington, 2004).

Without the systemic containment of an overall organizational framework that is consistent in its understanding of the needs of vulnerable people, we see professionals—themselves competent and concerned individuals—acting as if they are suffering short-term loss of memory. They live for the day, overwhelmed by the complexity of what is being asked of them. Those working to sustain and develop services for the elderly and other vulnerable people—with an emphasis on continuity and consistency—can be excused for thinking that they are counter-cultural in this society.

Note

1. I am grateful to Jonathan Gosling for drawing attention to this iconic figure.

CHAPTER SEVEN

The isolation of care services

I'm an old woman now
and nature is cruel,
'Tis her jest to make
old age look like a fool.

"Kate", in Gladys Elder (1977)

There are increasingly problems of relevance in using such much-handled and well-worn concepts as hospital and community. An important distinction is to be made between exclusive services that take the patients out of their existing social networks—for example, often when they go to hospital—and inclusive services that support patients in their social networks. But though hospitals have specialized and expensive plant, they are not the bounded institutions that they sometimes look. They consistently interrelate with other local social systems (another way of talking of community) that include other health systems. The resulting networks of care are thus going to touch at several points within a continuum of more or less exclusive and inclusive resources. Even more confusing, many "community" services—for example going into a care home—are likely to be as disruptive as going to hospital. With the closing-down of much institutional care, community became for a time a god-word: we were expected to abase ourselves before it and not ask what it is (Bell & Newby, 1972). Unfortunately, one consequence has been that we continue to give things a community label that disguises their exclusive characteristics.

The concept of patient-centred care has become devalued. King's Fund research investigated reactions of hospital staff to the concept of patient-centred care (and basic care, person-centred care, personalized care, dignity and respect, humanity, and customer care): "without exception, these words provoked either mixed or negative reactions" (Goodrich & Cornwell, 2008). Recently, exploring a new culture of performance management in social services, I was looking at the care for older people with cognitive impairment in a day-centre setting. There was a change from a day-care focus on activities alleviating social isolation to targeted programmes addressing issues of dependency. The primary task of the day centre was repeated and insistently described both by staff and management—emphasizing that they are activity-focused, with programmes designed to meet identified needs.

Need was defined in terms of a rehabilitative ethos, and maintaining independent living. This was then contrasted with the continuing dependency demonstrated by physically and mentally vulnerable and socially isolated service users. The task was often defined as what it is not—for example, we are not a day centre; it is not what people want, but what they need. This approach, while it is consistent with government policies relating to care in the community, does not address the dependency needs of service users, when needs (in particular psychological needs) are redefined as wants, which are then discounted as of lesser importance.

The staff knew about the cognitive impairment group that also met at the centre. Some of them also worked with this group. Not all, though—not, for example, the driver/carer who related to the clients all the time through banter, as these clients did not respond and were not rewarding for him. But some others got a certain satisfaction out of working with this group.

I observed how these clients were kept locked away at all times, out of sight of the main centre. They had a separate entrance, so that others never had to come across them during the day. They could not use the same dining room, or the same toilets, as other users of the building. It was explained to me that they were not to be disturbed, else they would lose their focus. There seemed to be an exaggerated fear of their running way, or exposing themselves to other clients, or other fantasies about the severely demented.

In making a determined attempt to get away from a traditional day-centre culture—which was thought to be passive and dependent, though the building had been full of lively interaction, according to legend—the service is attempting to apply a hi-tec ethos to a lo-tec activity. So all tasks are written down, routinized, Bingo (a social activity and very popular) being replaced by Snakes and Ladders (which is thought to be more developmental), allowing for very limited autonomy of staff in making and sustaining relationships with service users. Many staff are not themselves convinced by the primary task, as described above. They find it infantilizing of service users and themselves.

I sat at lunch with the group—one woman repeated again and again, "Very quiet here, isn't it!" At home, she said, there were three generations of her family at meals. I later saw an old man, himself uncertain on his legs, get out of his car to open the door gallantly for his wife, this same woman, as he took her home. The respect shown to the service users was evident, but the protocols were very limiting, with the exaggerated sense of the need to segregate these users, which would seem to promote an attitude towards dementia inappropriate for those living in the community and the professed ethos of the unit of maintaining independence.

A series of Tavistock Institute health care research studies were, on the face of it, studies of aspects of institutional life—focusing on a geriatric unit, a mental handicap hospital, a psychiatric hospital, and a children's ward in an orthopaedic hospital—but we did not see hospitals as unified institutions, closed systems, that we could understand without reference to their environment. Moreover, these were not straightforward organizational studies to do with creating a product or delivering a service. If an organization is characterized by a division of labour and unity of control, then the hospitals that we studied can only be said to have got it 50 per cent right. Unity of control is just not possible.

Every enterprise or institution has many tasks, not all of which are equally acknowledged. For example, a hospital treats patients; it provides employment for a variety of staff; it may train doctors and nurses; it may conduct or provide facilities for research; and this is one of the institutions in our society that has the task of helping to deal with the chronic problems of debility and disability, dying, and being bereaved. In a hospital the task of giving treatment does normally have priority, and if it ceased to perform that task, it would no longer be a hospital, as we currently understand the concept. But in general those institutions that offer help of any kind, physical or spiritual, find that their intake or their output or both may be intractable to control, and a hospital is no exception (Miller & Rice, 1967). That is why, in the continuing revolution of the NHS, acute hospital trusts are still particularly liable to create financial deficits, which a new generation of primary care trust commissioners may feel that they are struggling to control.

We should acknowledge, therefore, that it is difficult to manage the boundary between hospital and community systems of care. Management of a system is concerned internally with regulating its activities and externally with regulating its relations to other systems in such a way as to get its task performed. Similarly, overall management of the institution relates the constituent systems to each other and the institution as a whole to its external environment. Management is thus essentially a boundary function, at the time of both admission and discharge. The discharge of patients from hospital may, paradoxically, be experienced as contributing to a breakdown of health care and invalidate the good work done in the hospital as a community system. In such ways, the difficulty of managing boundaries leads to the making of difficulties in transactions between systems of care with exclusive us-and-them characteristics.

Public and private sector organizations have in common the experience that the demand for their services and products does not stay constant. Helping institutions are striking examples of those social organizations that may find their traditional clientele has gradually disappeared and that now feel inadequate to face the different and more challenging demands made of them. Care systems for the elderly manage their own boundaries to ensure the most effective use, as they see it, of their own resources in relation to the needs of an ageing population. They come into open conflict despite, or even because of, their mutual non-aggression pacts in defining areas of responsibility, because the different systems of care—which are both complementary and contradictory in their aims and definitions of task—attempt against all the odds to retain some semblance of a steady state (Schon, 1971).

We have seen already that elderly people in hospital are of three kinds—those who get better, those who die, and those who neither recover nor die. For the latter cases, the hospital has a clearing-house function, holding the patients indefinitely unless appropriate alternative care may be provided. In our study of geriatric hospital care (Dartington, Jones, & Miller, 1974), we examined, by participant observation and intensive interviews of interested parties, what happened to two sets of twenty patients admitted consecutively to two geriatric units. Eleven were discharged from a geriatric hospital to care systems different from those from which they were admitted. The hospital, in working towards the discharge of patients, was confronting community support services with issues of both accountability and competence to cope. Families often had long experience of "bearing the brunt", assuming responsibility and responding to need. But the family might expect that the temporary responsibility taken on by the hospital would become permanent. Supportive work within one care system was consequent on rejection by another system. But who decides the levels of tolerance in each case?

Of course there is cooperation between seemingly independent systems of care. The resolution of conflict may be achieved by *quid pro quo* arrangements, including the exchange of patients. Transactions across boundaries, however, tend to have an all-or-nothing quality that does not properly allow for mutual cooperation in dealing effectively with multiple aspects of the care of a disadvantaged group, where rehabilitation follows rejection and rejection may follow rehabilitation. Each system is defined by the making of a distinction between it and the other, between what it does and what is the responsibility of the other. In our study, such was the nature of the split between hospital and community.

Transactions are going on all the time between and within each of a range of different care systems, and each transaction is making a difference to all the others. The referral process is a serious exercise in collaboration between caretakers of the same or different disciplines, in the interests of furthering the welfare of those for whose benefit they have skills, training, qualifications, and resources that they may make available. In this, the referral is very different from an instruction. It is communication between two or more systems of care that are mutually autonomous. But the outcome may be the sharing or transfer of accountability for the treatment and care of a patient or client. Increasingly, this is in accordance with guidance from the Department of Health in determining, for example, eligibility for NHS continuing care. As such, the referral process is a mechanism for the deployment of resources.

I have described a health care system as an open system with inputs and outputs. It is, first and foremost, taking in more or less ill people and then treating and discharging them as more or less well people. If "more or less" sounds vague, we should remember the important middle range of those who are neither going to die in the short term nor really recover. The significance of this middle range varies with the specific task of the health system. It is not such a significant issue in the management of a maternity service, whereas it is in geriatric care, because ambivalence towards the objects of care would seem to correlate with uncertainty about outcome.

Referral in the middle range is an attempt to get an output by transfer within and between care systems. In the hospital that we studied, there were 1,094 admissions involving 840 patients in a 12-month period. Of these admissions, 29 (2.7 per cent) remained in the hospital for more than 52 weeks. The others died or were discharged home or to other care systems. This compared with the situation 15 years previously, where 221 out of 268 inpatients at this hospital had been bedfast for more than a year. A dynamic approach to geriatric patient care had transformed the nature of the throughput of this hospital. Also, as it moved from a custodial to a therapeutic model of care, it emphasized, as never before, the significance of making transfers across the boundaries of the system of care. The concept of progressive patient care was essentially about the transfer of patients within and between systems.

The admission of the patient to the hospital was itself the outcome of a transfer from community systems of care. The GP who made the referral was the representative of these systems. Referral is most definitely about making demands, and the GP often acts as interpreter for the family in its demands . Here is an example from our study of geriatric admissions.

> Mrs F, aged 82, lived alone. Her son and daughter-in-law lived about ten miles away. Her neighbours "are willing to call in and see her very regularly to check that everything is all right" (Medical Social Worker's report).
>
> After a previous hospital admission she was receiving some help, Meals on Wheels, with support from the district nurse and health visitor.
>
> The GP referred her to the geriatrician with a request that she attend the day hospital. This request was turned down, "as shifting her is liable to increase her confusion".
>
> Mrs F, in her precarious social situation, had poor eyesight and suffered from shortness of breath, exacerbated, according to the GP, by her tendency to panic.
>
> Mrs F's son thought that it would be best for her to go into residential care.
>
> The GP arranged an emergency admission to the general hospital. She was then transferred to an acute geriatric ward. She agreed to go into residential care for "convalescence" and after three weeks was discharged there from the hospital.

Working towards an admission to hospital for the patient, the GP may be relieving the family and also neighbours, and of course himself. But this is not the same as saying that the GP was pressing to off-load his patients while the hospital is resisting all-comers. In some instances, the GP might be very reluctant to let a patient out of his care. The geriatrician might be equally loath to delay the admission of a patient. From the hospital perspective, however, it was not possible to admit all patients referred to it, and there was natural resistance to those referrals that, in the context of the hospital's own set of therapeutic priorities, may not be well founded. This then illustrated the laws of the welfare jungle, where there were tests of eligibility within eligibility. Negotiations were idiosyncratic to the circumstances. The terms of reference were not spelt out. They became more intelligible when one understands how there were different expectations of the functions of the hospital by those working there and by others involved in the care of the elderly.

In talking with GPs we got the impression of their battling against odds. This was consistent with a pervading culture among those whose job it was to care for disadvantaged populations. This atmosphere—of dealing at second best, of being forced into almost unacceptable compromises and solutions, of choosing between two evils—was described well enough by the GPs themselves. And yet they were still expected to carry out their apostolic function, as if they knew what was right and wrong for patients to endure and should convert their patients to their own faith. They recognized that associated with the medical care of the elderly were problems related to their social isolation and potential rejection. Referral to the geriatric department was therefore a different issue for most GPs than a referral to the general hospital. We found that a GP might feel uneasy at referring one of his elderly patients to a general hospital, that this was an inappropriate referral, although he knew that in an emergency his patient will be admitted. So he would rather see himself as a supplicant to the geriatrician. But it is evident that he was interested less in consulting the geriatrician than in getting his patient into a hospital bed. Trained in a scientific discipline and experienced in the efficacy of social forces, the GP lived in two cultures. It is not surprising if sometimes he seemed to talk with forked tongue.

Sometimes it was quite explicit that a patient was to go to hospital because of a breakdown in alternative provisions, as in this example from our study.

Miss G, aged 94, had lived in a voluntary old people's home for 20 years. Because of financial difficulties, the home was to be closed down and the surviving residents, with the exception of Miss G, placed in local authority residential care.

Miss G took to her bed and, being bedfast, it would not have been possible for her to take a place in a local authority home even if she had wanted it.

The social worker of the voluntary home did not know until the evening before the day the home was finally to close what was to be the outcome of negotiations between the local authority social services department and the geriatric hospital.

Miss G was admitted to the geriatric hospital as a social admission for a limited period of ten days, while arrangements were finalized by relatives a hundred miles away for her rehabilitation and for further care.

The GP thought this was a satisfactory outcome, but he had been unable to resolve the issue of what was to happen to Miss G. From his point of view, someone had to look after her. He regretted the protracted negotiations.

The GP knew about the deterioration in the health of his patient; he also knew about the crisis in the family or a neighbour's distress or a breakdown of social services. Sometimes he relieved the situation by arranging admission to hospital. This was responsible and effective but was only partly to do with the medical condition of the patient, yet that was the primary concern of the hospital.

It was uncontroversial to state that a proportion of geriatric admissions were "social" admissions, though it is more accurate to say that a proportion of factors leading to any geriatric admission were "social". But the social admission, where these factors are dominant, is a way of taking pressure off another system of care. The treatment is effected by the removal of the patient to another system. The family get over their crisis, neighbours sleep better at nights, and social services continue to provide a range of services to some of those who need them. But we have also seen that an outcome of the referral process is the transfer of accountability. This may mean that an admission of the patient to hospital is a relief to the family, social services, and so on, but it is not then a stimulus for the start of their preparations for the planned return of the patient from hospital. After all, they are experiencing how they can get along better without the patient and not how they are going to continue to cope with the patient into the future.

Mrs S, aged 80, had lived with her daughter and son-in-law. After a fall the GP arranged emergency admission to the general hospital. She was going to be discharged home after one week. Her daughter was in ill health, and the son-in-law protested against the proposed discharge.

Mrs S was instead transferred to an acute geriatric ward, where she made slow but enthusiastic progress towards mobilization and rehabilitation. Her family visited her regularly and said that they were looking forward to the time when she would be able to return home.

However, the progress she was making on the ward was not sufficient to satisfy them that she was well enough to go home. She became somewhat depressed.

Her GP expressed his concern on behalf of the daughter. He supported the reluctance of the family to take Mrs S home at that time.

An attempt to discharge Mrs S was unsuccessful. The son-in-law wrote to the geriatrician: "To have Mrs S back here is crazy ... put her in any home you wish, but certainly not in mine."

Mrs S was transferred to the continuing-care ward, and arrangements were made for her to go into local authority residential care.

Those working in the hospital recognized, of course, that social factors were important, but as they were working in the hospital their primary task was still the treatment of sick people. The medical staff whom we interviewed agreed on the need for a socio-medical analysis of the circumstances of each patient and a treatment strategy using relevant data generated from both sides of the hospital gates. The dynamic concept of making positive therapeutic interventions as the most effective use of the hospital resources for old people included recognition of the social factors that precipitated admission and, in turn, facilitated their discharge. Nevertheless, the initial diagnosis and treatment clearly had a medical rather than a socio-medical basis, and social factors assumed greater importance only after treatment has been undergone and progress identified. Only then did the possibility of discharge of the patient become the more immediate concern of the hospital staff.

In this way, a discrepancy emerged between what was the overt task of the staff working in the hospital system and what appeared to happen to the patients at different stages of their treatment during the stay in hospital. The implication was that the community systems of care really should have the potential to give the overall care that is required, so that the hospital could simply treat the medical conditions as presented through the referral process, but that the community systems were somehow failing in their task.

Thus many of the difficulties illustrated in our case studies arise from the relationship of the hospital with its environment and are, to a great extent, outside the control of the hospital system. Hospital staff may try to build up a socio-medical picture of the patient prior to or at the time of admission, but there are many forces combining to diminish the picture to a narrow, more purely medical perspective. By the time that the patient actually enters the hospital system and takes on the role of patient in an admission ward, we are seeing the culmination of a process in which a person has come to fit a set of medical criteria for admission to hospital. The information about the patient is inadequate, patchy, and inconsistent, and the medical staff are more encouraged to reach their own conclusions primarily on the basis of their own examination of the patient in the hospital. All these factors therefore lead to a situation in which the initial diagnosis tends to be more exclusively medical than anyone, including the doctors, would want, and so is the treatment strategy deriving from this diagnosis. All efforts are concentrated on trying to build up a picture of the incapacities and capabilities of the individual as a patient in the hospital environment. Initial treatment objectives and strategies tend to take the form of, "We must get him walking", "We must stop her vomiting", "We must do something about her incontinence". And the medical staff have to ask first whether the patient is going to live, not where.

The referral process has already excluded the social factors, which were the initial impetus of the referral. We still have to explain the sometimes striking lack of information often held by nursing staff on hospital wards. In our study they might not know for some days who were the relatives, whether the patient lived alone or with his or her family, what had been the physical environment of the patient and how this contrasted with the physical environment of the hospital ward. This lack of knowledge, though dysfunctional to the maintenance of the individual's identity, is functional for the hospital in carrying out its immediate therapeutic task. For the moment, the only environment that matters is the hospital ward—anything else is confusing and disruptive.

This might not matter, but people do not fit exclusively the different kinds of care available. The clinical teams in the hospital themselves acknowledged that it is difficult to differentiate between those admitted primarily to access residential care and those returning to the community after a successful medical intervention, although there were great differences in the resource implications, and my observation was that both staff and patients were aware of these implications.

> Miss G knew instinctively what to do when she was faced with a threat of closure of the voluntary home: she became bedfast. After her admission to hospital, the staff there became aware of her social circumstances and were made uneasy. They saw her as a dignified old woman and did not think it was suitable for her to be on a geriatric ward.

Patients' fantasies in the 1970s of the hospital as a work-house were reinforced by underlying perceptions among the staff that admission to the geriatric ward represented a failure of external social systems. Feeling sorry for Mrs G was experienced as disturbing and distracting from the therapeutic task.

The external or "community" systems in turn corroborate this perception of their own failure. But patients themselves, or their families, may prefer to pretend that their problems be seen exclusively in medical terms and so deny and suppress the possibility that they are looking to go to hospital because of a breakdown in the support system around them. Acknowledgement of such breakdown may be tantamount to acknowledging some failure in the social inclusion of the patient himself.

Note

I first described the Tavistock research in this and the next two chapters in "Fragmentation and Integration in Health Care: The Referral Process and Social Brokerage", *Sociology of Health and Illness*, Vol. 1, No. 1 (1979), pp. 12–39.

CHAPTER EIGHT

Mediating between systems

Do not face them when they are on a high hill.
Do not go against them with their back to a mound.
Do not pursue them when they feign defeat.
Leave a way out for surrounded soldiers.
Do not block soldiers going home.

Sun Tzu

What happened to the family doctor? The traditional gatekeeper role of the GP may still be experienced in positive terms as the representative of community systems, acting as their interpreter and functioning as an editor of information. Information may be edited in different ways, most obviously by playing down or excluding altogether social factors known to the doctor and relevant to the total care of the patient, where such factors cast doubt on the likelihood of the hospital achieving an early discharge of the patient. Significantly, in our study (Dartington, Jones, & Miller, 1974), the family doctor played down what he most knew about—perhaps the social circumstances of a patient who has been on his list for twenty years—in favour of information that he associated with the specialist's interests and diagnostic skills. In this way he was feeding another's expertise, but at the expense of his own.

There is an important element of passive aggression in such a referral. The referral process is often about having one's fight and avoiding it. Apparently the GP was doing the right thing, making a medical referral. The aggression was in his motivation, which was to relieve a social situation.

This experience of the medical referral has been felt often enough within the profession. For it is by the use of edited information in the referral process that patients are admitted to hospital for medical or surgical treatment without proper regard for the complexities of their disability or are assigned to a lower order of care or even put into critical situations to force others to act, perhaps by sending someone out of hospital to an untenable situation and aggressively refusing to take responsibility for the consequences. But referrals from other consultants could cause the greatest friction. In the end the specialist may feel that he is the guardian of the dirty, the deteriorated, and the socially outcast, and he himself feels isolated.

The referral process allows for these attempts at dumping—and we will return to the theme of dumping later—because it is a translation of the circumstances surrounding a patient from a set of criteria suited for one care system to another set of criteria suited to another care system. This is a mutual activity between the two systems.

> Miss A, aged 80, lived with her two sisters. In this case the GP made a referral emphasizing the social factors. He described Miss A as a cantankerous old lady with two cantankerous sisters, and himself as the nut in the nutcracker. He had listened to the complaints of her younger sister and resisted pressure to make a psychiatric referral. Instead, he made a request to the hospital for the social admission to a geriatric bed.

> While Miss A was in hospital, a diagnosis of arteriosclerosis was made. It was agreed that she attend the day hospital after she had gone home.

Miss A was then admitted to an acute geriatric ward from the day hospital. The doctor there made a diagnosis of carcinoma.

A process that began with a referral for social reasons ended with the admission of Miss A to the hospital for medical investigation. Miss A died in the hospital five months later.

I have described the referral process as a mechanism of the deployment of resources by transfer between care systems. The phenomenon of edited information is part of a distancing effect that is created between care systems, and where this happens I have categorized the relationship between care systems as aggressive dependence. We can now see how this contributes to the all-or-nothing quality of the transactions, the dumping of problems (and people) from one care system to another.

The distancing of a hospital from the community where both patients and staff come from is not idiosyncratic to one or two hospitals. If so much conscious effort is often put into breaking down this distancing effect, it is because of the significance of the separation of hospital and community. In studying a more custodial institution—a mental handicap hospital (to use the language of the time)—we looked at the boundary between hospital and community by seeing what happened around the holiday admissions of children (Jones, Dartington, Hilgendorf, & Irving, 1973). These planned admissions were arranged with the social services department. They gave useful clinical surveillance for the children and relieved the families, but we found that the way these holiday admissions were managed needed some further explanation. First, though there were frequent intermittent transactions between social services administrative staff and the hospital medical secretarial staff, this mechanism seemed to be designed to limit communication between the two care systems. Second, hospital nursing staff did not expect to see the families of such patients during their stay. The distancing between those doing their best in different systems allowed them to maintain a disaffected loyalty towards each other. That they were highly critical of each other was beyond doubt. The criticism, more often based on fantasy and jealously protected ignorance than on the reality of the care, allowed them to continue to make use of each other anyway. Those families who saw enough of the hospital to be concerned for the welfare of children more used to a home environment did not make a fuss. They saw these repeated holiday admissions as the premiums of an insurance policy. They hoped that in this way their children would be acceptable for permanent institution care when the parents were unable to look after them. This was another aspect of the disaffected loyalty that was at work in the relationship between systems.

This example from a custodial institution demonstrates the antagonism associated with the dependent relationships between different systems. Where the patients or clients are themselves very dependent, so are the care-takers. In each case the dependency is put across in quite an aggressive manner, in effect saying that the dependency is not to be taken advantage of. Such total institutions as homes for the severely disabled may operate a horticultural model emphasizing achievement of the inmate who is "really normal" (Miller & Gwynne, 1972). People who are very heavily dependent on other adults for everything in their daily lives—being fed, being toileted, being washed, for being got up, put to bed and so on—may be seen to have more aggression than others to control. But the "inmate" has then to hold back his aggression, in responding to these insults to his autonomy, or this will be subsumed within his supposed pathology—the reason given why he has to submit to such a regime of care—for example, because of his "challenging behaviour".

The more custodial the institution, the more the aggression is about the maintenance of intact boundaries, both of the individual and of the institution, against the outside world. This aggression is evident in any dependent relationships between systems; the aggression that we see characterizing the total institution has found an outlet in the potential for transfer of accountability between care systems. Another example of geriatric care:

Miss E, aged 87, lived alone. Confused and with deteriorating health, she was admitted to a general hospital and transferred to an acute geriatric ward. She objected to being kept in bed and took to wandering. The need for constant supervision was a drain on staff resources. When she disturbed the consultant's ward round on her sixth day on the acute ward, an attempt was made to discharge her to a psychiatric hospital.

The next day she was returned from there. A second attempt on the same day to discharge her to the psychiatric hospital was successful.

Miss E had been admitted first to the general hospital. At the time of her transfer to the geriatric ward, the general ward sister warned the geriatric ward sister that Miss E was obstreperous. Through a series of rejections, the GP arranged her admission to hospital, and at the second attempt Miss E was found a place in the psychiatric hospital. Each transfer was made when it became clear that the previous system was not only unable but unwilling to cope. In this way, Miss E became eligible for psychiatric care.

The process described earlier that is labelled "referral" could in reality often be better described as disposal, where referral may be observed to be not so much the referral of the problem as the dumping of a person. There is a splitting-off of what are perceived to be undesirable aspects of the situation of conflict, retaining for oneself the good aspects and disposing of the rest where one can.

There may be quite vigorous testing of criteria of acceptability between interested parties, and a GP recounted to us a rather bitter anecdote:

A patient in hospital was visited by a friend from his church. The nurse on the ward asked the visitor whether, as the patient did not have any relatives, he would agree to be put down as next of kin, and he could then be informed of the patient's progress. He agreed and was later informed that the patient was ready to be discharged to residential care but that there was no place as yet ready for him. The friend was then asked if he himself would take the patient back to his own home for a short while until a place was available in residential care. He agreed to this plan. He understood that the patient would be staying with him for a week or more. He did not realize that the patient was doubly incontinent. The patient was discharged from the medical ward and arrived at his friend's home in an ambulance. He immediately defecated over the floor. The friend, who now had the systemic status of relative or of "loved one", contacted the hospital but was told that the patient was not an acute medical problem. He was advised to contact the geriatric specialist. There was no bed available at that time for the patient in the continuing-care ward. The church then attempted to arrange residential care for the patient, but their voluntary home could not cope with his high dependency needs and so returned him to his friend.

The GP gave the friend his advice; he suggested that the patient be left at the police station, and the police would then be able to arrange his admission to hospital.

His friend could not accept this solution. He looked after the patient for four months until his medical condition deteriorated further, so that he again met the medical criteria for admission to hospital, where he then died.

This anecdote stands as just one example of how tough the negotiations between care systems can become. Of course, what is striking about this story is that the carer was a friend and not a relative. If he had been kin, there would have been no story. However, it gives an insight into the reasons why the negotiations between care systems become so tough. There is a powerful element of moral entrepreneurism. Professionals have a language that defines their perception of role; so they relate to "patients", "clients", "service users", while families, as they describe it, have "loved ones". There is an assumption here of an emotional attachment that is both positive and to be respected. Those working in health and social care are reminding themselves, in using this phrase, that there are ties of kinship that they have to acknowledge, while they go about their business of making decisions. But, as we have seen here, "loved one" like "carer" is not a status to be taken on without thinking of the implications in the minds of professionals.

Those who have the responsibility of making the final distribution of health and welfare resources—for example, a panel that determines whether someone is to receive NHS continuing care—are interpreting, on behalf of a wider societal dynamic, what are the norms of social responsibility. It is not surprising that the exchange is sometimes abrasive, for agencies are telling the public and each other what they should be doing.

There appears to be an unconscious wish to act out the insolubility of an intractable problem—that people get older and weaker—by taking sides, even when this becomes dysfunctional. While each of these systems seems to be carrying out its task in a reasonable way, the care given to the elderly is undermined, and they are allowed to be pulled this way or that as unresolved conflicts get fought out almost literally over their bodies. The lucky ones are those who most easily make the transition of fitting one set of criteria of acceptability perhaps in community systems of care, to the next set of criteria of hospital care, to the next set—and back again. So this account of the referral process leads us to look again at the care systems and how they see themselves.

The more a social problem seems to be intractable, the more the specialized agencies mobilize to counter its effects on their preferred ways of working. This is a problem that has not been addressed in the inquiries that follow the failures of mental health and child protection services. Cooper and Lousada (2005) have described how a patient may become a non-person, where the care in the community system was "stuck with a patient whom they could neither discharge, nor for whom they could easily attract professional interest and support, where the manager of one system was unable to have a dialogue with the manager of the other" (p. 122). The problem is fragmented, its intractabilities split off and projected from one agency to another, like an intrapsychic game of pass the parcel. It is necessary then to understand how the different agencies determine what they are there to cope with, what they are not there to cope with, and how they tell the difference—for the definition of task seems to be a defence against the twin pressures of omnipotence and guilt. Moreover, the creation of grey areas of responsibility or of gaps in what used to be known as the welfare net is consequent on this process of defining task.

The pressures to be omnipotent are pervasive. In psychoanalytic discourse, there is a distinction to be made between "fantasies"—we are aware of those—and "phantasies", more deep-seated in our unconscious experience. We may need to inquire, fearfully perhaps, into the phantasies of omnipotence, childhood phantasies of destructive power, because—and this is the good news—we may see also how these are defended against in a number of reparative ways. Doctors and nurses and others who seek to sustain life and care for those who are debilitated and damaged are reparative objects in omnipotent phantasy. But we also look on them as if they are responsible for the damage, which they then have to try to do something about. The forms that this takes are many and varied, so let us take an apparently trivial example from everyday experience: A geriatrician hesitated about going into a ward for a brief contact because he would then have to shake hands with each of the patients on the ward—it was expected of him. Doctors are often seen as fatherly scientists who know what they are doing; nurses are firm but kind; social workers can get things done. However differently people may experience these types in reality, they still think of them as they ought to be, according to these prejudices. So the pressure is to live up to one's type.

In health care, as in the rest of life, our motives are thus not exactly as they seem, and there is collusion to maintain semblance at the expense of the reality. Every time a doctor insists on his clinical responsibility for his patients, he must know that his clinical freedom is severely constrained by the realities. The scientist has to give way to the pragmatist, but only with caution does he admit this to his patients. The social worker should know something about manipulation; it is his daily experience in his working life. The nurse serves God and Mammon—the doctor and the patient—in a world where tender loving care can sound like a death sentence and rehabilitation can feel like attempted murder. The doctor does things to patients that, if he were not a doctor, would be criminal. The other professions are not far behind in the legitimized deviancy of their interference in people's lives. But these privileges are paid for in the expectations that people have of them.

These are sufficient reasons why care systems have to be managed in such a way as to give protection to those working in them, and in particular to protect them from the worst hazards of their guilt about their phantasied omnipotence. This is done by making sure that they do more than they should, while surrounded by others who are doing a lot less than they should. Definitions of task are then a way of keeping down to manageable proportions failure, guilt about failure, and hence stress.

In discussing definitions of task, we may distinguish between what we ought to do (the normative), what we think we are doing (the existential), and what is actually going on (the phenomenal)

(Lawrence, 1977). These distinctions help to explain how we have grey areas, indeterminate areas of need that seem elusively not to fit within the task of any systems of care, for these grey areas lie between the normative and existential boundaries of these different systems. So we think we are having to cope with meeting needs although we should not really have to. It is then very difficult to sort out what we are doing.

To understand this, we must explain the tendency to put limits on the normative task. We are talking here of something that may be very commonly observed.

"He shouldn't really be with us at all . . ." "It's not really our responsibility . . ." "We are not really supposed to . . ."

The implication of these statements is that what we ought to be doing is less than what we think we are doing. The normative task ensures that we are, in our own eyes, doing more than we should. This is what happened with Miss E.

Miss E was transferred from the geriatric department to the psychiatric department where she was given the status of "guest", and returned to the geriatric department. The argument went that the geriatric department should not have to cope with a confused patient, and the psychiatric department should not have to cope with an elderly patient who is also physically dependent.

In defence of both systems we have to say that the geriatric department does not have the resources to contain a confused patient, and the psychiatric department does not have the facilities for physical medicine. To challenge this normative definition of task is difficult. We are back with the problem of managing resources.

"We look after people who have nowhere else to go." While this kind of statement should give an insight into the normative task of an enterprise—what they think is their special competence that they should be exercising—actually it more often gives a clue to the existential task that they think they are actually doing, which is more than they should: "This unit was not designed for incontinent/confused patients." But we just heard of the system of care that it thinks of itself as the end of the line for their patients, so there is a paradox of expectations.

It is difficult to get a good view of this process because of the distancing that I have described between care systems. But it can happen, for example, even between two wards in the same hospital. In the hospital where we were researching, patients who survived their initial stay in the admission ward of the geriatric hospital were transferred to the rehabilitation ward. Over time it was noticed that the patients on the rehabilitation ward were becoming more physically dependent. The doctors tended to blame the nurses for the declining quality of nursing care. In turn, the rehabilitation ward nurses blamed the admission ward for having done an inadequate job. Our observation was that patients were being shifted from the admission ward because these beds were needed for other patients and not because they were ready for rehabilitation. But both medical and nursing staff showed great reluctance in acknowledging this. No explicit policy decision was made to lower the criteria for transferring patients for rehabilitation. The rehabilitation ward nursing staff made no direct protest to the medical staff about the de facto change in criteria. Of the twenty consecutive admissions to the hospital, at least four were clearly transferred from rehabilitation for reasons of expediency. However, each was treated as a temporary exception to the regular rule, thus perpetuating a particular pattern of conflict.

The effect of thus deliberately maintaining ambiguity about the appropriate boundary management between the admission and the rehabilitation wards offered an alibi that related to the patients who were the failures of that care system, the patients who would neither die nor recover. Where there is ambivalence about aims and uncertainty about outcome, those working in the different subsystems were nevertheless able to be surprisingly specific about definitions of task. According to those definitions of task, they were doing more than they should be. But the explicit task seemed to contract down to describe only part of the work experience.

This defining-down of the task is a symptom of stress. We believe conscientiously that we should only be doing so much for such and such a group, but look how much more we are being asked to take on. Even when we realize this is happening, criteria of responsibility are not adjusted to take account of the new reality.

We do not get rid of the cuckoos from the nest, nor do we really admit them as legitimate. This same ambiguity serves again as a defence against the quite unrealistic expectations that we have of ourselves. The normative task is defined down, as within a closed system, as if it is not subject to vagaries of the environment. The existential task is opened out, as if the system is being flooded by the environment. In the perception of those that live and work in them, care systems are inadequate to meet the challenge that face them, but it is not their fault.

So what is actually going on? There is a reversion towards stasis so that the phenomenal tasks of the different systems take account of most of the people in need. This is worked out by complicated and subtle checks and balances, and the results may look haphazard. Patients are not always discharged from hospitals when they are well enough to go. Families often do not reject their sick members, though they may be ill-equipped to give the 24-hour care that is required. In our study, residential care workers accepted that the cost to them in having a deteriorating patient admitted into an acute hospital bed was that they would be asked to accept a more chronically long-term dependent patient from the rehabilitation ward, a process that contributed inevitably to the increased overall dependency of the care home residents. In these ways the phenomenal task of one care system more or less fits with that of another. But, as we have seen, the management of grey areas is the occasion for inter-group activity and conflict, where the opportunities for compromise are severely constrained by the all-or-nothing nature of the transactions.

CHAPTER NINE

The case for integration

I know the joy of fishes in the river
Through my own joy, as I go walking along the same river.

Chuang Tzu

This account in the preceding chapters of the interaction of care systems has reached a depressing stage with the description of conflict and mutual lack of understanding. But as this is an account of fragmentation and integration as countervailing pressures in health care and as we now get to discuss integration, we have come to the crisis point, where we can look for signs that there could be a better outcome.

The various systems of hospital and community have tasks within an overall common objective of health care. Liaison and communication are ways of relating between systems. They also become urgent and necessary when there is any discordance between systems. We are talking here, though, of the integration of tasks so that what the family does fits with what the hospital does, and the social services area team, and so on. We have seen that care systems tend to be consecutive in their operation, and this reduces the overlap of accountability that goes with concurrent activity. The consequence, moreover, may be the development of whole areas where no one wants to be responsible. Integration involves the taking back by different care systems of those parts in themselves that have been fragmented and projected outwards as being the responsibility of others.

The hospital, for example, may be one in a succession of systems of care, so that the GP does not visit his patient in the hospital; the social worker or the residential care worker who do visit may feel that they do so more as friends of the patient, as visitors, than as co-workers with the hospital staff in his treatment and care—like the GP, they are accepted in this role much later, perhaps at a case conference to promote the imminent discharge of the patient back to the other systems. In this way the individual patient or client passes through one care system to the next. The referral process as we have described it sees that he fits the criteria of each in turn. He is ill enough to be admitted to hospital, where he is rehabilitated well enough to go into residential care. The all-or-nothing transaction requires that certain aspects of patient care be a primary task at this or that stage of his progress. Moreover, the translation from one stage to the next may be disruptive and abrupt.

In an exclusive care system, transactions across the boundary of the system would be concentrated at the beginning and at the end of the treatment process. Interest shown in the treatment process from other care systems would be experienced internally as interference. An inclusive system, in contrast, would need to maintain continuous transactions with adjacent systems. A coalition or temporary task system of representatives of the different interest groups would mean that "admission" and "discharge" could be defined as a readjustment of the level of involvement of different systems with the patient's progress. The patient would not simply be transferred from one system to the next.

My observation is that care systems are sometimes more exclusive than is claimed for them. Those who complain that their organizations or institutions are isolated, that their work is unsupported and not understood, may also be those who behave most as if they are working in "silos" or closed systems.

Thus we found in our study of the mental handicap hospital (Jones et al., 1973) that direct links between what were seen as alternatives—community-based support and institution-based support—were controlled at a series of checkpoints that only the patient himself was able to pass through. The social worker who transported short-term patients to and from the hospital was not the social worker of that patient or his family. The social worker did not visit the hospital at any other time—only to deposit or collect the patient. GPs were expected to examine their patients before admission to the hospital, where the patients were then again screened in the medical ward within the hospital, so that sometimes they could take part in the normal social life of the hospital for less than half of their stay. Patients brought few personal possessions beyond their clothes and often, indeed, wore hospital clothes during their stay. Ward staff knew about the patients from their previous stays in the hospital and not about what had happened to them between admissions. When long-term patients attended outpatient clinics at other hospitals, they were escorted by junior nurses unable to give information about the patients.

This was more than a temporary problem of a lack of communication. There were always good reasons for each of these instances of the maintenance of a seeming impermeability of the hospital boundary. In general, though, this is a phenomenon where the hospital interacted with its external environment so that its actions might be internally consistent, but the relevance of these internal activities to other systems of care was not easy to test. For all its open systems characteristics, this was a centripetal or inward-looking system, so that the potential complexities of contracts between hospital and community were simplified and stereotyped.

But we may think that the hospital was not really so isolated. During the time of our study there was a new appointment at the hospital, that of community nurse. A social work unit was set up in the hospital, and this was staffed from and responsible to the local authority social services department. Less formally, nurses took patients into the local village and had always done so. The education department made use of local educational facilities. The children's ward set up a parents association. Where there is evidence of fragmentation, one may also expect to see such compensatory pressures towards integration.

Likewise, hospital care of the elderly shows multi-organizational characteristics. For example, a patient was discharged home to the care of community support systems, but these included return visits to the outpatient clinic at the hospital, which thereby gave access to the hospital's specialized resources alongside the community-based care systems.

Patients may be expected to be ambivalent in their attitudes towards illness, both accepting and rejecting some aspects of what this means for them. Less obviously, perhaps, those who look after them also take ambivalent standpoints about their own dependency and autonomy in their working relations. Much as the patients' ambivalences can be used to fit them to this or that care system—by the selective presentation of one side of the case—so the care systems may be selectively presented as being more or less fragmented or integrated in their inter-organizational dynamics. Thus, if feeling under attack about deficiencies in the care provided, it is natural to argue that one's own agency is unsupported and isolated. But also, if challenged about being isolationist, it is equally possible to put forward contrary evidence of mutual participation with other systems in health care provision. In looking now at the integrative process, we have to ask if this selective use of evidence really demonstrates that there is as much mutual participation as it suggests.

For example, the domiciliary visit by the old-age consultant may be seen as a community service across the institutional boundary; or is this just another checkpoint in the process that the patient has to go through on his way into hospital care? In our study we observed how a GP was not present at the consultation, and the only question that the geriatrician was really being asked was whether he was prepared to admit the patient to the hospital beds he controlled. A complex interaction of different interests may be narrowed down in this crucial pre-admission period and experienced as a simple interaction between primary and secondary care systems. This may be a convenient way of looking at it, but, as we saw in the use of edited information, it is not really the whole story.

But if integrative processes are not all that they seem, why is there not more conflict? I have argued that the conflict is defensive, protecting against failure to live up to omnipotent fantasy. As such, it does not always have to be acted out but may be expressed in other ways. It is possible to be much more cooperative than one lets on and so to retain an aggressive stance and yet work effectively with others. The denial or displacement of conflict has to be understood in the context of family, social services, health services, voluntary groups, and so on that are actually caring and need each other. So the representatives of the different systems of care put a significant emphasis themselves on the importance of personal contact in their work. The old-age consultant knows certain GPs better than others; perhaps he or she gets on with the social services assistant director in the local authority. Or, a residential care worker has a lot of time for one doctor but none for the medical profession. These relationships are rightly felt to be important because they override the defensiveness of the different systems. The splitting and projective mechanisms of inter-agency relationships are powerful, just because they are fantasized, and so they can then become weakened through the reality of one person knowing enough about another to trust them. These relationships lead to the development of informal and sentient-based task systems that straddle the boundaries of what might otherwise seem more like warring factions.

We may position care agencies along an exclusivity–inclusivity axis, with the vertical axis showing where they fit along a warehousing–horticultural continuum. After studying institutions for the care of the elderly and the mentally handicapped in the 1970s, we have seen how they were already moving from a custodial towards a therapeutic model. It would be wrong to suggest a simple correlation that custodial institutions are exclusive and therapeutic institutions inclusive. For example, the kind of therapy being considered may be as important as the organizational context in which it is delivered. There were interesting indications from a study of a psychiatric hospital that a ward organized for medical servicing is more likely to show evidence of the split between hospital and community services than a ward operating a more social psychiatric approach to treatment (Towell, 1975).

One test could be of the quality of the transactions at the beginning and end of each care cycle. As patients were recycled through different and apparently autonomous support systems, we could see that the slower the operation of this cycle, the less willing was each independent system to take on the patient and the more difficult it became to get rid of the patient. We have ourselves seen that families who have looked after their own elderly relatives for a very long time are expected, just for that reason, to be able to continue indefinitely in the same way—though the logic of that expectation is not evident.

The integration in health care must involve a sharing of resources, including human resources. The wide-ranging organizational changes in health and social services may even be having an interesting effect among the less obviously expected outcomes: the attempt to fit highly rational but theoretical schemata to the historical realities means that new responsibilities criss-cross somewhat haphazardly with old sentient boundaries and open up opportunities for a more mixed economy in the provision of resources. Individual treatment strategies may be seen as an alternative to batch processing of patients. The important difference is that the individual has a unique relationship to his or her environment. In batch processing the environment is a constant—the hospital ward, for example—and patients are suited to their environment (otherwise they should not be there!). As we have seen, unique environmental factors are screened out as the individual becomes the patient. If this screening is not done the individual has still to be thought of as having his own world, his own environment, of which the hospital ward now becomes a part. The radical significance of this different approach is shown by comparing Figure 9.1, where the individual (I) is processed through a series of care systems, with Figure 9.2, where we see the individual in his environment. It seems that the multidisciplinary team already exists as objects in the individual patient's world and only needs to be discovered for themselves

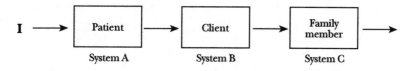

Figure 9.1

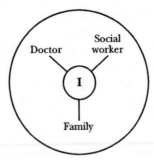

Figure 9.2

by the people involved! We can see how the care of the individual patient is managed by people who come from a different care system. It may not be so readily apparent that they set up their own temporary organization to do it (Figure 9.3).

We are here describing a transitory task system that has come together around a particular treatment programme. It survives only as long as it is needed and draws its members from different agencies, each with their own ways of working. At the same time, it has an existence independent of its constituent parts. An exchange has taken place, and now care-takers are acting in roles that would not be possible within the pre-existing systems. This last point distinguishes a transitory task system, a truly multidisciplinary team, from a collaborative process, where there are professionals who remain in role within their own agencies and interact procedurally across their respective boundaries.

In a research study of the children's ward of an orthopaedic hospital (Dartington, Henry, & Menzies Lyth, 1976), we were look-

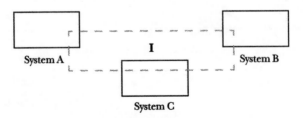

Figure 9.3

ing at ways in which the psychological needs of very small children might better be provided for in the hospital ward. There were some changes in organization derived from an appreciation of the needs of the children, but this further involved a reappraisal of the social realities of the hospital. The experience of the staff was transformed, as was that of the children and their families. The mothers of the children were integrated into the new ways of working, and this helped everyone to cope with the discontinuity between the "special" care of this institution and the "normal" care of the family. Maternal presence became a major factor in the management of the care of the children in the ward. We may see how the mother was herself an active member of the transitory task system to do with the care of the child. In this way it was possible to extend and develop the roles of the mothers and also of staff, who were working with the mothers in providing treatment and care for the children. Although this was a hospital ward, a family member or a social worker might have authority within the transitory system to retain an appropriate responsibility for the care of the patient. The environment of the patient was then, in psychological terms, not bounded by the hospital ward.

With the temporary task system, I am thinking in terms of an interactive organization-in-the-mind, of which the case conference is only the formal expression. In contrast, in the study of geriatric hospital care, the case conference was very much part of the management of the hospital system, specifically to do with managing the discharge of the patients from the hospital. Social workers present saw their job as dampening down the enthusiasm of the doctors to discharge patients. When the senior doctor was not present, the social workers themselves took on a more aggressive stance in pursuit of this task. It was an interesting group dynamic, but it was less about therapeutic need than it was about the survival of the hospital system through the effective movement of patients. We may compare this with the system that evolved in a psychiatric hospital, where a charge nurse and a local authority social worker jointly managed the admission and discharge of patients in a geriatric ward (Savage, Widdowson, & Wright, 1979).

So transactions between care systems do not have to have the all-or nothing quality of the referral process as I have described it. We can now begin to think about an alternative way of looking at these transactions, by looking further at the management of transitory task systems.

If the referral process is a linear way of negotiating between systems according to an exclusive model, how is it different when the interested parties retain their interest in working together? We need a concept of social brokerage. It is not a new idea that people need an interpreter or even an advocate to help them pick their way through the complexities of statutory interventions in their lives. Less formally, we often go for advice to those we think of as being accessible. This might be to those who have authority to be effective on our behalf, but very often not: the receptionist rather than the doctor, the nursing assistant rather than the ward sister. These friendly but sometimes unreliable spokespeople help individuals to cope with the strangeness, to them, of helping agencies and institutions. But we are still talking more of symptoms to the problem than of solutions. The problem is that the individual would find it difficult at the best of times to relate to these systems and, as a patient or client, is having to make the attempt at what is a very difficult time to be properly assertive in his or her own interests. We have had our attention drawn to the need to protect the rights of those who may be admitted to hospital for psychiatric reasons. Is it possible that the physically ill need similar protection—for example, if they are elderly and likely to lose their "rights"?

The role of social broker is open to anyone, but it does not fit easily with having an interest in one or another of the options. Thus a GP or a social worker might see him/herself in this role but can only carry it through imperfectly. Perhaps it must always be an imperfect role while the individual progresses through a number of interdependent but separate support systems, for it is the job of the social broker then to keep the options open. As in geriatric medicine so in social work there is a move to take a more interventionist approach to the problems of old people. While it may be argued that it is natural and appropriate that the social worker takes on an interpretative or protective role, this may not be possible if the role is that of case management (e.g., resource management). Where there is evidence of the existence of a transitory task system around the individual, the social broker role is to manage that transitory system and may be carried out by a number of the participants.

Such systems involving professional workers might then be thought to replicate the neighbourhood networks through which people's needs are met informally. Thus we find there are networks of people in different systems, and these relate in an informal way. It then becomes a bit more realistic to think in terms of a social diagnosis, so that help is made available when it is needed, now and in the future. What is screened out through formal organizational design and the defensive use made of organizational boundaries is retained in the informal networks and brings into the strategic plan what at the time may be thought of as extraneous or irrelevant to the current problem. The significance of informal channels of information must be evident to anyone working in hospitals. The question is, why is important information retained in formal systems and only passed on in this way? Our examples of the children's ward and the psycho-geriatric ward were exceptional in the institutionalizing of the transitory task system. What we are calling social brokerage then becomes a part of normal management functioning, as it is about making the space within which the individual can best relate to his or her environment. The temporary task system, where it exists, does not always become so visible.

The mother gives this kind of protection to a small child, and in the children's ward this is one reason for not separating the mother from the child at times of stress. But this is not exclusively a parental role. It is more what may be thought of as a "dependency-object role", which could be taken by, for example, a health visitor or a social worker as the patient moves through the various stages of being admitted to and discharged from institutional care. In this way the emotional needs of the individual are met, at least to the extent that there is some continuity and consistency in an unstable environment. But emotional needs are not only met in a static way of being around the patient, and the dependency-object role is an active one and has the potential to exercise considerable leadership in the management of the care of the individual. Case studies of school-age volunteers visiting old people demonstrate how natural is this development of befriending into an active role (Dartington, 1971).

Social brokerage, unlike referral which tends to fit the individual to the resource, is about the integration of resources around the individual and maintains the individual in relation to his or her environment. This is essentially a pluralistic approach to the management of health care and, as such, is always under threat of demarcation disputes and envious rejection of good practices.

There is also evidence that innovation and change can be stimulated by the sharing of experience and mutual support between systems. In different ways those managing care systems may seek to extend their representative roles. A group home of people who made the transition from psychiatric hospital to community was managed by a voluntary organization, a local Association of Mental Health (Dartington, 1978). The committee included a consultant psychiatrist, an assistant director of social services, a GP, a nurse from the hospital, and so on. They were there not as representatives of the division of psychiatry, the social services department, the family practitioner committee, the division of nursing: they did not have formal authority in that way as representatives of other systems; rather, they were there in their own right as members of this voluntary association. As they were not there as managers of resources other than those of the association, they were now in new generic management roles in the transitional task system of the ex-patients/residents of the group home. As members of the voluntary organization, these professional workers of different kinds were interpreting their own care systems to the people who were making the transitions between them. This is another example of social brokerage out in the open. But those involved had found a different place from their own agencies to do this work, and as such it is again an example of deviant organizational practice.

The Dementia Care Strategy, promoted more recently by the Department of Health, includes a recommendation for the development of a dementia care adviser role (Department of Health, 2009). Not themselves responsible for the provision of services, advisers would act as a single point of contact for people with dementia and their carers, providing advice and signposting them to the care needed. But social brokerage is not easily given an organizational legitimacy. There is a reason: its task is to integrate different resource systems in the environment of the individual. These systems have the task of managing their own resources. Social brokerage may, perhaps, then be described as the acceptable face of role taking, for it implies an easing up of professional care-takers' defences, where they take risks with their—in two senses—contracted role in the management of limited resources. Put another way, they put a different emphasis on their sense of responsibility. They are working in a diffuse situation: they have to be confident that they know what they are doing; with an understanding of the phenomenal task, the professional in role can demonstrate this self-realization, like any individual, in maximizing their potential through mature relationships with others. In the end, integration of health care requires that the care-takers are able to work in such a way that they do not insist that their split-off part of the process is a world of its own, to which others have to adapt. Integration is about making a society fit for the most vulnerable members of that society—the ill, the disabled, the disadvantaged—to live in.

Like all ideas, that of social brokerage is more in accord with certain values than with others. It has more appeal for those who are sensitive to evidence of creeping totalitarianism in the most benign institutions than to those who have an implicit trust in rationality and efficiency and see these as sufficient checks to abuses against the individual. We may say that care systems should be fit for purpose for those being cared for. It gets more and more difficult if one has to look for alternatives to alternatives and make an indeterminate number of linear transitions in the process in the hope of getting a better fit for the individual with a challenging environment. But, as we have seen, that is exactly what can happen.

CHAPTER TEN

Human nature
and organizational change

> The sense of oppression no longer sprang exclusively from a
> psychic situation but from concrete reality . . . I had to try and
> understand what had happened and to what extent my own
> experience coincided with that of man in general.
>
> C. G. Jung

I have run out of ways of saying we are in a new situation of
greater complexity, confusion, and incremental change than
ever before, while at the same time acknowledging that the sun
will rise tomorrow as it did today. It may be true—but then again,
when was it not true? However, I also like the idea that we do not
always want leaders who know exactly where they are going. We
also need leaders who want to find out where we are going.

As a consultant to organizations, I like to be reflective but I
also want to be useful. So what has this got to do with the state
of mind of those that I consult to, when they get up on a Monday
to start another week's work? My proposition to start with is that
there is an inherent struggle between our innate desire for stabil-

ity and containment in managing our experience of work and our desire, which we associate with our professional identity, to make a difference.

There are times, often on Monday mornings, when we hate change. I want to hold open the possibility, taking the risk that I will be associated with the dark forces of conservatism, that there are even times when it is all right to hate change—as long as at the same time we also acknowledge our experiences of others, and how we feel about them, when from our point of view they are being negative and obstructive, when we are frustrated and fed up with the inability of others to see that their lack of imagination and jobsworth mentality is getting in the way of what we are wanting to do.

It is a difficult dilemma that we face. We need to accept that we are having to survive in a turbulent environment and that our evolution as social animals—where we are still, in our individualism, at odds with our groupishness—is slow and painful and lagging far behind the immediacy of the changes that we are facing and making.

The social scientists who introduced the idea of the turbulent environment were dismayed that we snatched at the phrase without waiting to understand the thinking behind it:

> values are psycho-social commodities that come into existence only rather slowly. . . . For a new set to permeate a whole modern society, the time required must be much longer—at least a generation, according to the common saying—and this, indeed, must be a minimum. One may ask if this is fast enough given the rate at which Type IV [turbulent] environments are becoming salient. [Emery & Trist, 1965, p. 31]

And that was back in the 1960s, when—from a contemporary standpoint with a poor sense of history—the world was young.

So without being judgmental, or taking sides, we have to understand the battles that go on in the workplace between the commitment to values, which are historical and therefore backward looking—to do with the desires we had in committing ourselves to this or that training and subsequent career decisions—and the commitment to new certainties, which are immediate and untested and political.

Over a period of eighteen months, I attended weekly meetings of a community mental health team (CMHT) How was I to understand the sense that I had, in agreeing with the management team in an NHS Trust that I and colleagues would consult with the CMHT, that I was being thrown to the wolves?

We were working from the premise that a reflective stance would be helpful in working with intractable problems—in the individual, in the group, and in society at large. We were on the side of human nature, you might think—and we did not think that this positioned us as being against organizational change. The CMHT was working very much with some of the more dysfunctional aspects of human nature. The NHS Trust itself was suffering under a projected £2 million deficit, which the chief executive blamed on the high cost of agency nursing and social care staff and locum doctors. We might ask, though, was the work so destabilizing that it was difficult to recruit and retain a skilled and qualified professional workforce?

As organizational consultants, we were quite as convinced as the management of the need to achieve a change of organizational culture to achieve the desired integration of health and social care in the delivery of services. And yet, as I say, our experience was that we were thrown to the wolves. We were to be thrown to the CMHT to be savaged, while the management hurried on. The middle management, trying to live with the anxieties of their chief executive, were themselves fearful of what they were managing, because they did not believe it could be contained or constrained into the realities of their management imperatives. They were, I suggest, fighting human nature rather than working through people to meet their objectives. This splitting, when it happens, is so obviously destructive of effective management that we have to understand what makes it pervasive in the NHS at this time.

Organizational change, in the sense that I am thinking of, is a response to an external opportunity or threat. It is rooted in the cause of doing things better, of improving on current performance. There is so much of a continuing attempt at change in the NHS because of an increasingly powerful tendency to move away from a spiritual or fatalistic acceptance of morbidity and death and, instead, to find fault with an incompetent management. Acts of God, by definition, do not involve liability, but we have created any number of authorities on earth that we can berate with our thwarted desires, and the NHS is the example best known to many of us. We have now arrived at a situation where national politicians know that they are going to be held accountable, in an imprecise but real enough way, for the next flu epidemic—in fact for any mortality, general or specific, in the electorate. It inevitably follows that there is an anxious political engagement with the management of our health services; it is worth remembering how this is a relatively new phenomenon.

There is nothing more stressful than being held responsible for something you cannot do much to influence or help. High levels of stress have been found in manual workers and long-distance truck drivers and the like as much as in senior executives, who can at the least exercise their authority in the belief that they are doing something about the mess they can see all around them. But, in the situation I am describing, managers at all levels are themselves now being managed in ways that they are experiencing as being their worst nightmare—a shaming and not-to-be-confessed sense of their own impotence.

We were always going to have problems when performance indicators were transposed into targets. For example, a reduction in waiting lists is a useful and important indicator, one among others, of a well-managed, flexible, and responsive service; but when it becomes a target, backed by punitive sanctions, then the process is distorted, leading as much to the possibility of abuse as to improved quality of service to clients and patients. Managers begin to display all the symptoms of performance anxiety, and—another sign of the adolescentiation of society—they massage the figures as a way of keeping up to expectations.

This is the context in which I observed the tensions experienced by the different professionals in working in the CMHT. After working with the team for some months, meeting with them weekly to discuss issues of common concern to them, I reflected how one of the community psychiatric nurses in particular had described himself as an old lag. It was an interesting phrase, implying that he was in some way a recidivist offender. But what, then, was his offence?

There are ways in which an emotional world—in this case, the emotional world of people with severe and enduring mental illness—seems to infect all who come in contact with it. It is not just that it arouses transferential responses in ourselves—it can also elicit a parallel emotional process, mirroring and enacting the worlds we are in contact with.

> The team got angry about management and resentful of them—resentful at times of any authority other than their own, as if this were a world that was potentially hostile unless proved otherwise. At times they seemed to welcome the opportunities to talk; at other times, not—very much like their clients.

I have reflected on my part in this. I turned up, tried to be reliable, tried to be consistent—quiet virtues that are becoming rarer in an organizational world of electronic time management. I had the intention to be responsive rather than impose an agenda. I also followed my own principles of professional practice—meeting regularly with colleagues to share our experiences and think about what was happening in our work with those who are described, according to a military metaphor, as front-line workers.

Despite my good intentions, I felt increasingly uncomfortable. They felt I was being imposed—the managers said it was for me to work out my own agreement with the team. So I was identified with a management but without authority: I begin to experience the impotence for myself.

I wanted to say to the old lag: if ever you are worried that we might be management spies, forget it—I would certainly not have reported about what went on or was said by individuals in the group discussions, but the sad fact was that the managers were not interested in hearing anything of my experience or overall impressions of the CMHT system. If they had been, my thoughts might be summarized:

- That the teams have developed a siege mentality, as a way of coping with the demands on them, coming from an environment that is also perceived to be under siege. So they gather themselves to fight back but not always effectively. This is seen in the relations of teams to management, and the teams experience management as vulnerable to their attack. Team managers have been unhappy in their roles, bridging the professional/ management aspects of their work.

- That there is a definite sense of retreat, with the loss of key staff in teams, and an increased pressure on team managers, that it is all down to them now.

- That management often has to work through negotiation, and this is appropriate. But at times management here is seen to *exist* by negotiation. (An example in the CMHT had to do with team members sharing the load in relation to intake. Introduced with a long process of consultation, leading not to such a great impact on the work of teams, but apparently to very different ways of doing this between teams, and now to be subject to review. Review may seem to be an alternative to or postponement of decision-making.)

- That there is a separation of leadership and management—so that it is also difficult for managers to be seen to give leadership. It is difficult for managers to tolerate the fact that others cannot stand being managed—not to attack back, but also not to give in.

- That teams have a nostalgia for a fabled past, when there was professional leadership and not such a need for management. Leadership is more partisan than civic—for example, it works better within rather than across boundaries of professional and agency identity.

- That at times it seems that teams resist both leadership and management. They need leadership to feel they are a team; however, that can also feel intolerable, because then they have to acknowledge differences. The differences are not simply between professional groups, but expose other issues—for example, those who are thought to be pulling their weight more than others in taking on and working with difficult cases.

- That sometimes, more in the state of mind of a defensive fortress rather than an open system, team members and also managers demonstrate a commitment to grievance, seemingly always complaining. This has a deadening effect, so that no one listens and there is very little linking of experience.

A report with such content would not have been irrelevant to a wide range of interventions with health care systems at that time. Thinking again of the old lag, one thing that he and his manager could agree on was this—that he was difficult to manage. He was negative and uncooperative, but he was also representing an important truth about the depression and sense of hopelessness of the work. His clients depended on him, and they also hated him. One of them was threatening to murder him. At times he and his colleagues were seriously frightened by their clients, but some things are not to be spoken of in meetings. He lived with the pain all right, and found his own ways of survival—by going sick, protecting his work load, taking it out on his own organization rather than the client. In this way he became identified with the client. They were both against the system, which was about order in the face of chaos and so could not fully recognize what it meant to be truly vulnerable.

Living with vulnerability means accepting and understanding one's limitations and yet continuing to live in an area that is unsafe. Clients and professionals both know about their limitations, though they both also often have to act as if they do not. In clients, this is called pathology: in workers, it is professionalism.

They are then subjected to what is in effect a normalization programme, which in the case of the CMHT means that they are asked to work in a multidisciplinary team. They are being asked to give up the defences that are their own carefully worked mechanism for surviving, and with no promise of any better support in place of these.

In this context, we have to think about how organizational change is experienced inside the system as imposed from outside in response to an external opportunity or threat. We may even have the sense now also that the organizational change is introduced because of a basic mistrust of human nature, out of a mistrust of the ordinary dynamics of person on person, system on system, and their capacity in time to work things out. Organizational change is then not so much introduced as induced, to hurry up a recalcitrant human nature, that in the fantasy of modernizers would stay in the womb if it could.

I witnessed a fierce exchange between managers and front-line workers during another consultation with a social service department:

> The front-line staff said that the assessments being made did not include the assessment of needs for which there was no possibility of provision. I would have thought that quite likely— even sensible, from a certain perspective. What was remarkable was the anger of managers about this proposition and their determined denials that this was happening. They had to believe that all unmet need was being accurately recorded. Unmet need that they did not know about was intolerable. If they did not believe their own statistics, they would be overwhelmed by the enormity of failed expectations. And yet at others times, in the privacy of their own company, these same managers would comment on the stresses and absurdities of the monitoring fever imposed by an anxious political leadership.

At such times, one becomes very aware of the Janus-like qualities of modern management. Janus was the Roman god of boundaries—hence January as the first month of the year. He had two heads, so that he could both look out and look in. So I think he makes a good image for the manager, who is always working on the boundary of the enterprise, creating and maintaining the conditions in which work can be done. According to mythology, before Janus there was Chaos, which we may think is somewhat harsh as a description of the NHS before general management. But my observation of the manager is of someone who is not two-faced in the bad sense but who actually does have a perception of two worlds, the one rational, clear-headed, and numerate, the other complex, contradictory, and resistant to quantification.

There has been a shift in the process of dependency within systems, as they have developed a culture of psychological self-sufficiency. In the weakening or destruction of an external resource—the will of God, the good of the nation, the welfare state, the permanency of corporate life—in the experience of the employee there is still a lingering sense of failed dependency of institutions to contain the anxiety inherent in their work, as we have seen, and then increasingly of taking flight into a magic omnipotent fantasy or grandiose narcissism. The myth of infinite resource is maintained, but within a finite system.

While management struggles with the challenge of being truly Janus-like in these difficult circumstances, those working at the front line are likely also to be split between those looking inward to their professional competence and those looking out in a spirit of partnership and modernization. So we have the old lag, and the others, whom we might think of more as the ladies of the parish, enthusiastic and keen to support whatever new ideas the modernizing vicar has in mind.

Managers are known by their fruits, their individual performance targets. The faith of the modern manager is a forward-looking optimism, which is defensive against the anxiety provoked by thinking about chaos. But the manager has to look back, too. Leaders without followers do not get very far in the long run. Among their other qualities, they have to be able to use their sense of their own vulnerability. Larry Hirschhorn (1997) has described how, in contemporary organizations,

> the enterprise asks its employees be more open, more vulnerable to one another. But in becoming more vulnerable, people compound their sense of risk. They are threatened from without and within. . . . Thus the stage is set for a more primitive psychology. Individuals question their own competence and their ability to act autonomously. In consequence just when they need to build a more sophisticated psychological culture, they inadvertently create a more primitive one. [p. 27]

So, come Monday morning, the people I have been consulting to may continue to draw on their enthusiasm to make a difference, but I am suggesting that they also remember to draw on the experience of the old lag.

CHAPTER ELEVEN

True and false relationship in health and social care

People in a hurry cannot feel.

Paul Tillich

There has been a denigration of dependency in social welfare systems. At the same time, the importance of relationships has been devalued, apparently under threat from an individualistic approach to human relations—what in social policy is now called personalization (Duffy, 2005; Leadbetter, 2004). This policy initiative is intended to give people more control over the care they receive and who provides it: they are allocated a personal budget though direct payments and given help in making their own arrangements. The approach has enthusiastic pioneering support—for example, through an organization called In Control.[1] This initiative is very positive in itself; my focus is on the context in which this is being promoted.

We live in a post-dependent society (Khaleelee & Miller, 1985), which has the characteristics of what has been described as a therapeutic state (Nolan, 1998). In this post-dependent world, authority is mainly internal and ahistorical, located in the individual self—for example, it is not externally represented by parental figures and intergenerational dynamics of tradition and innovation. For at least forty years we have been living with this so-called triumph of the therapeutic (Reiff, 1966), where there is arguably a new view of the self—I feel, therefore I am—seen as the touchstone of modern culture (Bell, 1973), but also a new justification for the state: as one headline put it, "We're All Sick and Government Must Heal Us". The state draws on the therapeutic as the dominant cultural system to justify its actions, but we may think that it is taking an increasingly behaviourist view of its powers of intervention.

This behaviourist approach derives in part from the very strong assumptive belief system that our actions are mostly instrumental and economically driven. The nature of man may then be described according to a resourceful, evaluative maximizing model, firmly centred in individual self-interest (Jensen & Meckling, 1998). This is the intellectual tradition that has led to senior executives being offered stock options so that they are fully committed to shareholder value and also, for example, to the internal market in the NHS—achieving results by competition rather than cooperation. However, a consequence of this socio-economic theory of man as a paranoid agent of his own self-interest is that the fundamental importance of dynamic relationships is discounted and discredited.

It is now our everyday experience to use the appearance of relationship to achieve a business objective—"have a nice day." This is services marketing, where the relationship is used to sell a product. This marketing relationship has become confused, I think, with what we may think of still as a therapeutic culture of person-centred added value. The therapeutic discourse is then not really about a dynamic understanding of people interdependently in relation to the world they are in; rather, it acts as a defence against that understanding. The therapeutic, as it is now understood, belongs to the tradition of the Kleenex and paracetamol, an immediate response to a recognizable problem. Every fault has to have a cause; every disappointment has to have a scapegoat. As a result, we are living with a distorted therapeutic vision of rights and responsibilities, the basis for a litigious society. What is missing from the debate is an examination of authority.

Where the therapeutic approach is shown to be weak is, for

example, in relation to what is now called the parenting deficit. The contemporary approach to issues of parenting is constrained by the language of (children's) rights and (parental) responsibilities. This is psychological silo thinking: look at the child over here, the parent over there. The focus is not on the relationship. But, in contrast, the psychoanalyst Donald Winnicott said that there is no such thing as a baby on its own, but always in relation to its mother, and a psychoanalytic approach might ask, what is the authority of the parent in relation to the child? Instead, there is a seemingly attractive focus on mutuality, but only to be understood narrowly in terms of exchange.

A supposedly therapeutic approach today to mental health is demonstrated also by the language of recovery. For example: "recovery is about people seeing themselves as capable of recovery rather than as passive recipients of professional interventions".[2] In 2002 the NHS introduced the Expert Patients Programme,[3] a self-management programme for people who are living with a long-term condition, with the aim of supporting people who have a chronic condition by increasing their confidence, improving their quality of life, and helping them manage their condition more effectively. The programme runs for two and a half hours a week for six weeks.

This emphasis on self-management has a lot of strengths—but I want to note also the diminishment in the importance of relationships to others, including a reduced respect for the authority derived from competence and experience of others. Why should I think that anyone knows better than me about anything? Is not the customer always right?

There are powerful managerial constraints on relationships within a therapeutic culture. One example would be the management of care workers in relation to service users.

A home care team, working in the community, is employed by the local authority. The care staff are contracted to work the time they have been allocated with each service user. The technology now allows for a home visit to be timed to the minute, and the management say that this way we can introduce some flexibility. For example, perhaps the service user needs more time on this occasion. The carer can give her the time, and we can monitor that and take back that extra time from the next visit. In this way, we are being more responsive to client need; in this way, the system is seen to offer more flexibility as a way of asserting more control.

The reality is that, left to themselves, some carers would do a lot more than they are contracted to do, because they get into a relationship with the service user. Other carers exploit any lack of surveillance in the system to do less than they might. That, you might say, is human nature, the good-egg/bad-egg syndrome. The response is to make them both the same, to contain the good and coerce the bad to a single standard of a National Vocational Qualification within a National Service Framework.

This is benign in its intent, but it is also Orwellian in its process. The only way it works with any humanity and respect for relationship is that it is applied in an inefficient and incomplete way. Some very good care is provided despite—not because of—these safeguards. Some bad care may also go undetected by the monitoring system.

Clearly regulation does not sit easily with relationship. Marianna Fotaki (2006) has drawn attention to "contradictions that are intrinsic to the policymaking process because in addition to their declared, normative objectives health policies also fulfil deeper existential functions in society" (p. 1726). What is spontaneous, idiosyncratic, uncertain in its outcome, does not fit with an agenda of national standards. If you allow carers to have relationships of any significance with service users, things will get messy. We need the remarkable competence of ordinary people to care for others, but then we become frightened of that competence and impose mechanisms of control rather than, in the supportive psychological sense, containment.

In organizational life, it looks as though relationships are all important, but this is expressed more through networks than sentient one-to-one communication. In public services, this is expressed through the use of "bank" staff working shifts as required.

In such ways there has been a collapse of respect for relationship. The therapeutic ideal turns out to be self-sufficiency, while a more relational or psychodynamic perspective is about our capacity to connect with others. As Fotaki (2006) observes, "the shift of responsibility for one's home healthcare to patients in effect denies their vulnerability and their need for care" (p. 1734).

I recently overheard in a café a woman who had been visiting her mother in an independent-living scheme. She was complaining vigorously that her mother was being forced to do things to demonstrate her progress in being independent—for example, doing the washing-up with two care workers standing over her—and she saw this as patronizing and insulting, more a punishment than support. When she complained to the manager, she was told that they had to show outcomes to justify their funding. I looked at the website for the care home:

> Our care homes provide 24-hour support and accommodation to people who are too vulnerable to live independently. We work to maximise independence and increase or reintroduce inclusion within the community.
>
> Following a shift in policy local and central government, several of our services are being re-modeled into supported living services or accommodation based services to better suit the needs of service users and meet the strategic plans of commissioners.

On the ground, it seems that this means standing over an old lady doing the washing up. In a care system of this kind, if a significant relationship does develop, this is likely to be deviant from the protocols.

Patients and clients have been re-allocated the role of service users, again to play down the dependency in the role and to maintain the appearance of an autonomous being. This is attractive as an attempt to ensure some parity in what is otherwise an unequal power relationship. It is the therapeutic equivalent of customer.

Customers are assumed to know their own needs—except that needs are better defined in this context as wants, subject to cost benefit analysis and open to substitution. Increasingly, illnesses are being linked to life-style choices: obesity leading to diabetes, cardio-vascular diseases associated with diet and stress, alcohol-related diseases, and so forth. Assessment processes therefore fit uneasily in this process. Assessment of need is, in fact, increasingly to be understood as the management of resources.

Does the service user fit the criteria for the provision of the service according to a rights-and-responsibility framework—for such-and-such a reason the user has the right to a service, and the provider agency is commissioned to provide it. Interventions are delivered and monitored as short-term interactions. Cases are opened, shut, reopened according to externally determined criteria. The apparent offer—the promise of a relationship—is a shallow pretence.

Psychoanalysis, in contrast, can seem extreme in its reliance on relationship. From the perspective of its critics, it does not seem a very efficient technique and is hard to defend as best value. A neutral observer might even think that the technique has become ritualistic and the purpose has been lost. But at the core of this work there is a respect for the patient's own capacity for learning and the difficulties of learning that contrasts with the urgency of time-limited interventions. The intimacy of a relationship requires an open-ended commitment, when you do not know exactly what you are getting into and what you will get out, but you have the capacity to stick with it. The turn to the relational in psychoanalysis has given fresh attention to the mutuality of the relationship.

However, the new therapeutic agenda, being more about self-love than understanding of envy or hate, is much more concrete and positive in its promises about outcomes, and this serves also to distract from the importance of inequalities. If we can be anything we want, it does not matter that we or anyone else starts at a disadvantage. The argument persuasively made about the correlation of economic inequalities with a wide range of social ills (Wilkinson & Pickett, 2009) does not get heard, it seems, and is drowned out by the opportunity agenda and the myth that we are all masters of our fates.

The fact that social mobility has decreased with the unleashing of market forces as the driver for change needs some explaining. It would seem that this kind of freedom—this entrepreneurial space—only suits a small minority of people, or a small part in each of most of us. The majority remains risk averse, having neither the stomach nor the skill to make the best of every opportunity according to a resourceful evaluative maximizing model. So the poor actually get poorer—the middle range, where most service professionals are found, more or less stay the same, and the "top" 1 per cent enjoy exponential increases in their wealth.

The employer–employee relationship, which is worked out also in manager–subordinate relationships at different levels in the organization, is increasingly understood to be instrumental. On the face of it, there is a more transparent openness, as described in the 360° appraisal process. There is also the possibility of evaluation of every kind of interaction. Enthusiasm—religious or secular—is not really welcome, because it is difficult to manage. The voluntary sector, with its not-for-profit organizations created and developed to give expression to deeply held values and commitment, is also continuously suborned by an insistent demand that the organizations become efficient, competitive social businesses. Chief executives move from one cause to another without noticing any conflict of interest, and, having successfully competed for government funding, they become government advisers.

But below that opportunistic leadership, people continue to act on their enthusiasms as much as their interests. A partner from one of the major consultancies described to me how the voluntary sector did not understand the employer–employee relationship. Volunteers, local committees, ideologically driven workers, have a tendency to do what they think right—so that managing them requires an empathy with the other's desires that can only be carried through by relationship—and if that breaks down, there will be trouble and conflict. Some political groups offer an extreme illustration of this dynamic. Voluntary organizations may be seen to implode, as they experience and react to injustice and persecution within their own membership rather than in the external environment.

We may think, in contrast, of traditional examples of relationships at work—the master–servant relationship and the craftsman–apprentice relationship. In each case there is a contract that acknowledges dependency in a way that is diminished currently in the employer–employee relationship.

The new working relationships that I have described are an attempt to realize a relationship without dependency—a relationship of independent operators who are nevertheless managed by surveillance and audit and a performance–related reward system. Qualities of loyalty and trust are no longer needed if their advantages can be achieved by technicalities of performance management.

The quality movement introduced the concept that nothing has meaning unless it can be measured. But now the concept has developed, so that anything that can be measured is assumed to have meaning. This has led to paranoia about the collection of data by commercial enterprises on their customers, by government agencies, and, of course, by employers on their employees.

This robotic tendency in human relations—to see the individual as a productive unit that can be made to run at near-optimum efficiency—contributes to the stressful experience of people at work, because they are not, in fact, robotic at all. To cover for this discrepancy, we have developed a thriving therapeutic culture at work, which addresses the needs of the human-in-the-robot—for example, counselling services funded by employers, and, for more important people in the organization, executive coaching. Employees who are downsized are offered out-placement services. Remuneration is increasingly linked to performance bonuses, as if the individual is a sole trader in a competitive enterprise.

The happiness debate, stimulated by Richard Layard (2005), has exposed the uncomfortable realization that increased prosperity has left us unhappy, experiencing the status anxiety and the affluenza that Alan de Botton (2004) and Oliver James (2007) describe in their interpretations of the therapeutic culture—as James says: "Consumerism is a skilful education in narcissism."

The problem with acknowledging dependency is that it adds weight to our responsibility for others without any corresponding gain of rights. A dependent workforce is understood to make the organization less competitive. And it can be argued, persuasively, that knowledge work requires less dependency in the workforce than, say, manufacturing processes. On the larger stage, it has been argued that a dependent population "looking for handouts" because they are sick or disabled makes a state economy less competitive in the global market. Such an interpretation by liberal economists has been questioned, as there is evidence also that generosity of benefits can also be linked to the lowering of unemployment rates.

We recognize dependency in the nursery and the hospice, but not in between, though it remains a fact that there is not a time when we are not dependent on others for our survival and comfort. The human need for relationship is not, of course, lost or destroyed in the meantime. As I have said, care workers may demonstrate very powerfully this capacity for intimate relationship outside of kin, even when the protocols do not allow it Following the dominant rational model of human behaviour, we act all the time as if we are on our own in our achievements, and we do everything we can to defend ourselves against the sure and certain knowledge that this is just not true. Or, as Sartre put it, Hell is other people. This contrasts with the Maslovian ideal of self-actualization, a sophisticated development of the notion of the self-made man, emphasizing individual achievement, including a capacity for relationships (Maslow, 1970). But hatred of dependency is different from denial. The hatred we can do little about, but the denial is something for us to work with in the development and management of human systems.

One place to look for answers would be the breakdown of community, of connectedness (Sennett, 1997). Robert Putnam (2000) analysed a culture of increasing social isolation in communities in the United States that seems to describe aspects of UK society so well that I think we are looking at a wider phenomenon, again linked to market economics, which posits an isolated paranoid individual negotiating his self-interest in relation to others, whom he imagines to be as isolated and paranoid as himself.

We may protest at times about the degrading of identity from citizen to consumer or customer. What sounded alien at first, awkward, a joke even, when we heard station announcers advise customers of the lateness of their trains, is now taken for granted—I am talking about this language of "customers", not the lateness. (Did I really hear of the lateness been ascribed to "a customer under a train"?) The change of language was deliberate and was introduced ahead of public perception of our changed relationship to public services.

We are not only customers, of course; for, as long as any of us are active at all in the market economy, we are also providers of goods and services. Our everyday experience of being both customer and provider is very stressful, and at times it may be toxic (Stein, 2007). We have to manage as best we can the integration of these oppositional positions—the relation, insofar as it exists, is instrumental, a defensive contract rather than a real engagement of identities.

The freedoms of the market are arguably good for us as customers but get us anxious, overworked, or feeling excluded in our roles as suppliers of goods and services. The force of contracts has replaced the power of relationships. We think that we are living in a therapeutic culture, but that indulges the fantasy of personal salvation without the necessity for a committed relationship and provides a very necessary defensive environment, psychologically speaking. In helping us to live with the freedoms of a market economy that leave us feeling entrapped, it makes the resultant world of targets and audit more or less tolerable (Dartington, 2009).

Notes

1. The In Control website is: www.in-control.org.uk
2. From the website for Re-think—Recovery: www.rethink.org
3. See the expert patients leaflet at www.expertpatients.co.uk

CHAPTER TWELVE

The costs of care

And so, from hour to hour, we ripe and ripe,
And then, from hour to hour, we rot and rot,
And thereby hangs a tale.

As You Like It

In 2007, an influential group of MPs collected evidence towards a damning report that highlighted the current state of dementia care in the United Kingdom (Committee of Public Accounts, 2008). Only a third of people ever received a formal diagnosis, and thousands of people were not getting the care and treatment they deserve. The stigma and misunderstanding associated with dementia was named by Professor Sube Bannerjee, taking the lead for the government on a new dementia strategy, when he described dementia in a newspaper interview as "quite an unattractive illness. It's seen as something dirty that should not be talked about."[1] In his view, the current system made it much easier not to be diagnosed than to be diagnosed.

At the same time, the Commission for Social Care Inspection reported on the inequalities in social care in this country (CSCI, 2008). Local authorities were making their own decisions how to interpret the eligibility of people for social care. This eligibility framework was set in 2003 by government, with its Fair Access to Care Services Guidance (FACS) promising that "Implementation will lead to fairer and more consistent eligibility decisions across the country". The guidance outlined low, moderate, substantial, and critical needs—and made the distinction, which they said would be helpful to councils, between presenting needs and eligible needs: by 2008 councils had mostly decided that needs did not start to become eligible until they were substantial—or in some councils already critical—and the government instituted another inquiry into the problem its guidance had created five years previously.

To meet low to moderate, and then substantial, needs would be supporting the independence of people living at home. Focusing only on substantial and critical needs requires by that stage more heroic interventions, including admission to residential care or hospital, because of the breakdown under stress of informal systems of care.

New initiatives were already under way—for example, an agenda to develop the personalization of services and the introduction of personal budgets. According to Alan Johnson, then Health Secretary: "Our commitment that the majority of social care funding will be controlled by individuals through personal budgets represents a radical transfer of power from the state to the public. Everyone irrespective of their illness or disability has the right to self determination and maximum control over their own lives."

Faced with a crisis of dependency, we may see how the response is yet again to create opportunity. It is to say to someone who is losing his or her mind, we will give you the opportunity to manage your own finances and in that way the market will provide for your needs. We are to look to the opportunities of the market, and not any more to a bureaucratic dependability—as was provided, for better or worse, through traditional social care arrangements with local authorities. But it is not new that social care has been means tested, and many people—in 2008, those with assets over £21,500—have already been paying for their own care, have already in effect been providing for their care through personal budgets of their own. And as yet, this has not created a satisfactory market of care that meets their needs.

The market that has been created, if we can call it that, is in informal care. In the United Kingdom, 6 million people are known to be unpaid carers, 1.5 million of whom are providing over 50 hours of care a week. The government recognizes, but not generously, the importance of this informal system of care, which in real terms is more than the whole NHS budget. In 2008, if you looked after someone for more than 35 hours a week, providing essential support for the activities of daily living, and had no other income, you were eligible for a carer's allowance of £48.65 (about a quarter of the minimum weekly wage at that time).

This is progress, if we think back to the founding in the 1960s of the Council for the Single Woman and her Dependents. The concept of carer did not exist then: the assumption had been that single women would look after their parents, reduced to poverty, without pension or security. In the next ten years we saw the introduction of the Attendance Allowance and the Invalid Care Allowance. At the same time, the disability movement made a powerful impact by moving from a medical to a social model of disability, not apologizing for being different, and in time making a great escape from institutional care. When the Tavistock Institute got a call from a Cheshire Home asking for consultancy, it was not from the management but the residents. What happened next was published in the book, *A Life Apart* (Miller & Gwynne, 1972). This study argued that the essential characteristic of the people taken into the institutions was not simply that they were disabled, and therefore to a greater or lesser degree in need of physical care, but that they had been written off by society—a social death, preceding by many years a physical death. The debate continues to develop, as the disabled people's movement looks to complete a further shift of focus from quality of care to quality of life (De Wacle, van Loon, Van Hove, & Schalock, 2005).

Those who neither die nor get better continue to represent a very great challenge to health and now to social care systems. There are ways of alleviating the problem. For example, closing residential care homes and transferring vulnerable old people has led to greatly accelerated mortality in those affected. In ten years (1984–94) geriatric hospital bed numbers fell by 33% and local authority home places by 41%. Independent (private) nursing homes flourished as a result, but in the next ten years local authority fees had been kept so low that private sector closures also became significant—in 2003, this equated to a loss of 1,000 placements a month. The Wanless Report, *Our Future Health Secured?* (Wanless, Appelby, Harrison, & Patel, 2007), found that both attendance at A&E departments and emergency admissions to hospital had increased by over 33% in recent years: "These dramatic rises are hard to explain . . ." And having arrived in hospital, older patients are of course particularly at risk from MRSA and *C. difficile* and similar infections.

There is a continuing controversy about the costs of social care. The NHS costs are estimated at £1.17 billion out of a total economic burden (e.g., including the costs of informal care) for late-onset dementia care of £14.3 billion (more than the cost of stroke, heart disease, and cancer combined) (National Audit Office, 2007). This is against a background where health care continues to be the government priority. Patricia Hewitt gave the annual Health and Social Care lecture[2] at the London School of Economics in 2005, in which she did not mention social care. She talked of

> the values of a health service funded by all of us, available to each of us, equally, free at the point of treatment, with care based on our need and not our ability to pay. These values are non-negotiable. They make the NHS unique—the institution that makes people proud to be British. They are a beacon of compassion and an ethic of care, of fairness and of social solidarity, mutual responsibility one for another, in times that so often feel harshly individualistic. In everything we do, in every change we make, we will not compromise those values.

Perhaps she felt that she did not have to mention social care in this context because she was Secretary of State for Health. In 1974 a reorganization of healthcare and social care divided the responsibility for the delivery of services between separate government departments, achieving a definitive separation of the heroic and the stoical in terms of policy objectives. Nick Goodwin, a senior fellow at the King's Fund, summarized the impact:

> The effect of dividing care services in this way, in the last 30 years, has led to the development of different lines of political

accountability, different and competing policy objectives, and different cultural and financial regimens. Budget separation for health and social services acts as a key barrier to integration as an economic incentive was created to shift costs from one organization to another rather than act in partnership. [Goodwin, 2007]

After further reorganization, social care has survived as a junior partner, with its separate budget in the Department of Health. Joint working between health and social care has been described as the holy grail, an aspiration throughout the history of the NHS. The Department of Health tries yet again, with "integrated care pilots". And the distinction itself is questioned—for example, by Professor Jon Glasby at Birmingham University: "I'm not sure the distinction was ever meaningful and it is certainly not meaningful now in an era of long-term conditions and changing demographics."[3]

In 1999 the Royal Commission on Long Term Care recommended that the costs of social care should be split between living costs, housing costs, which would be means tested, and personal care, which would be available according to need and paid for from general taxation. As the report stated, "this will ensure that the care needs of those who, for example, suffer from Alzheimer's Disease—which might be therapeutic or personal care—are recognised and met just as much as those who suffer from cancer" (Royal Commission on Long Term Care, 1999).

More recently, a report on the ethics of dementia care made the same point, that dementia is a medical disorder and the needs arising out of the disorder should therefore be met in the same way as those arising out of cancer: "In allocating resources, and in determining standards of care, it should make no difference whether the intervention is classified as 'health' or 'social'" (Nuffield Council on Bioethics, 2009).

However, this category of personal care was crucially undermined in a minority report to the Royal Commission on Long Term Care (1999), in which Joel Joffe and David Lipsey recommended that the state should make some contribution to nursing care but that personal care should continue to remain a means-tested benefit. As they said, they did not want to weaken the incentive for people to provide for themselves privately: "Just because much health care is free, it does not follow that personal care should be free too." In practice, this means that the nursing care of someone very dependent and living in a nursing home is likely to be calculated at just over £5,000 a year, while the current costs of means-tested social care for someone in the medium to later stages of dementia are running at £30–50,000 a year. The then Prime Minister Tony Blair announced, "We have chosen not to introduce free personal care because it would cost about £1 billion and we believe that the money would be better spent elsewhere."[4] That social cost was estimated to rise to £6 billion in 2020.

The problem has not gone away. Having consulted in 2007 on the development of a National Care Strategy, in 2009 the government began a new consultation, called Shaping the Future of Care Together, on reform of care and support systems more widely. It put forward several options: that there would be a state contribution of a third or a quarter of the costs, or people could choose to pay into an insurance system, or there could be a new comprehensive insurance system, over and above national insurance and general taxation, to pay for a National Care Service. However, none of the options put forward would allow for care funded by general taxation, and the housing and living costs of a care home—for example, much of the actual cost to those paying for the care—would not be covered (HM Government, 2009). A government proposal was put forward to offer free care at home for 400,000 of the most vulnerable older people: David Lipsey attacked this proposal as a "demolition job on the national budget".[5]

No wonder we have a fear of dependency. How can we bear to spend that sort of money on people who will not get better, who do not contribute to our competitiveness in a globalized economy? But is that reason enough to leave the problem with those who are most vulnerable? The informal care system does remarkably well, often with crucial support from health and social care systems, in which front-line workers—street-level bureaucrats (Lipsky, 1980)—bend the rules to meet the need. These services are constrained by the heroic imperative of making a difference, getting people back on their feet, while families and front-line workers (sometimes in collusion with their managers) understand that there are times when vulnerable people obstinately stumble into greater dependency.

The policy-making agenda is predominantly heroic, being driven by political urgencies. The stoical agenda is carried more by Janus-headed managers, looking both ways at economically driven targets and at the psychic pain of their client communities. Is it so difficult to think clearly about appropriate responses in such a context because we are experiencing a kind of moral panic, as if the elderly and the dependent are experienced as socially deviant in a culture of opportunity and enterprise?

In this difficult context, it is important to remember that the care of our most dependent people is often done very well. The scope and extent of informal care has demonstrated that an extraordinary commitment and perseverance of care is also an ordinary and everyday experience in very many families. The newsletters of voluntary organizations, blogs, and books written by carers (e.g., Whitman, 2009) are full of anecdotes of care driven by a natural altruism that put to shame the rational arguments of social policy. This altruism is not only in families, but can be observed also in many care workers, who bend and break the rules imposed on them by management systems that deliberately constrict and constrain services based on relationships. They are deviant in relation to the opportunity agenda in order to meet the real needs of those with whom they are working.

So what can be done? We must look critically at the social policies—and the management practices that derive from them—emerging out of a restless government programme of change, driven by anxiety about competitive advantage, and see how far they are supportive of the individual's capacity to accommodate changes towards greater independence, when appropriate, and also greater dependency, when this is appropriate. Getting the most vulnerable in our society to do what is needed to meet government efficiency targets will diminish the good results of the opportunity agenda. Isolating and undermining the human capacity to care for the vulnerability in ourselves and in others can only make us poorer as a society. But if we can overcome the moral panic and fear of dependency that drives policy, we might all sleep easier in our beds.

Notes

1. Interview in *The Guardian*, 13 February 2008.

2. The full lecture is available at: www.dh.gov.uk/en/News/Speeches/Speecheslist/DH_4124484

3. *The Guardian*, 9 September 2009.

4. House of Commons, February 2001.

5. House of Lords, November 2009.

PART III

THE PERSONAL AND THE PROFESSIONAL

CHAPTER THIRTEEN

An Alzheimer's case study

> . . . There are no gardeners
> here, caretakers only
> of reason, overgrown
> by confusion. . . .
>
> R. S. Thomas

In this third section of the book, I am now able to review my participant observation in a single case study, where a close member of my family became ill with dementia and the professional and the personal came together, as I worked with the neurology specialist, the family doctor, social services, different parts of the health service, and different carers, including informal carers (Dartington, 2008). My wife Anna wrote about her experience of developing Alzheimer's, and her account is included in the next chapter. This case study serves both to reinforce the learning about systems of care that I have described from my professional role in social research, and to take further the analysis of underlying societal, organizational, and individual dynamics of care.

Dementia—a set of illnesses of which Alzheimer's Disease is the best known and the most common—results from a physical deterioration of the brain, so that the synapses become dysfunctional, coupled with an accelerated dying-off of brain cells leading to shrinkage; the cumulative consequence is extreme cognitive and physiological impairment. The disease is often confused in its early stages with a depressive illness and in later stages with psychosis. The traditional distinction made between neurological and psychological explanation has, as Damasio (1994) argues, been "an unfortunate cultural inheritance that permeates society and medicine". In our society, dementia has succeeded tuberculosis and cancer as a symbol of the intractability of illness, having unknown cause and untreatable effect. An old-age psychiatrist has described the "major assault on our therapeutic narcissism" of dementia services, where the normative pattern of care—an intervention leading to recovery—is reversed:

> Working with someone with an irreversible illness may stimulate hostility, helplessness, frustration and therapeutic nihilism. . . . Unconscious determinants of our chosen healthcare profession may not be satisfied by patients whose condition is chronic, even deteriorating. . . . The patient who does not get better may provoke feelings of aggression and sadism accompanied by anxiety, guilt, depression and reparative wishes. [Garner, 2004, p. 221]

The lack of information about the conditions that seem to give rise to the incidence of Alzheimer's is almost intolerable, so that a succession of theories have attempted to make links with diet and life style. A famous study of nuns suggested that convent life had some significant advantages in this world as well as the next. They were an ageing population that was full of life. Their way of life was not itself a defence against dementia, but many of those who were found *post mortem* to have had advanced Alzheimer's had tested as mentally normal when they were alive (Snowdon, 2001).

Such a study is very encouraging in the context of a social model of disability, but traditionally those with such a hopeless illness would have been incarcerated in the back wards of institutions. This was the social death, which preceded physical death, that Eric Miller identified in relation to physical disability in the

1970s (Miller & Gwynne, 1972). The disability movement at that time, with its emphasis on human rights and the rejection of a medical model of incapacity, is a useful guide to thinking about other forms of discrimination and disadvantage. We may also think of other kinds of social exclusion, with our prisons full of people with mental health problems, and asylum seekers denied the opportunity to be other than criminal.

In contrast, in my own research on attitudes to disability (Dartington, Miller, & Gwynne, 1981) I was able to observe both the approach taken in a local authority care home—except that it did not call itself a care home but took its name from its address, like any other residence—and the leadership of the "officer-in-charge", though he did not call himself that. The care workers were encouraged to see themselves as the arms and legs of those who did not have the use of their limbs, but not to take over their minds, which functioned normally. Put simply, this meant, I will put your shirt on you, but you have to indicate which shirt it is going to be. This apparently simple practice involves a multiplicity of negotiations around the boundary of the self. For someone with dementia, whose mental capacity is under increasing threat, it involves the person in the care role acting as a mediator, not only in a practical way, but as a psychological interpreter, negotiating realities (A. Dartington, 2007; see chapter fourteen).

In bringing together the personal and the professional in this way, I am attempting an integration of my own that is itself very difficult to sustain. We like to know where we are with people. I am a social scientist; I am a family member talking about someone with dementia. These are different roles, though held by the same person, and the usual processes of fragmentation demand that the roles be kept separate. We have expectations of the patient or carer, and expectations of ourselves as researchers and commentators or perhaps as clinicians in relation to the patient or carer, and these expectations are very different.

John Keady and colleagues have argued for the importance of constructing care from an autobiographical perspective and integrating lay knowledge within an overall professional response to the family's needs (Keady, Ashcroft-Simpson, & Halligan, 2007). One of the uses of literacy is that older people, unlike infants, can describe their own experience (Athill, 2008; Hoggart, 2005). In this process of integration, I am helped also by post-modern vehicles for expression—for example, the blog on the internet. Over a six-month period I recorded some of my observations in the form of a blog. Here is an extract, in which I began by quoting the opening sentence of Franz Kafka's novel, *The Trial*:

> "Someone must have been telling lies about Joseph K. for without having done anything wrong he was arrested one fine morning" (Kafka, 1925).

> Anna keeps asking: What have I done wrong?

> The carer says that Anna is "going to panel" tomorrow.[1] We don't know what questions will be asked or answers given. This unseen tribunal decides what resources we may have or not.

> Coming back from a group relations conference, I realize that we are fearful of a management that hates us.

> (*Two days later . . .*)

> Anna was anxious first thing: she said, "I don't think that it's going to work."

> And that is the question now. I am worried that we will be losing the carers from the home care team—the framework on which we build all the support around Anna. While I was away, their managers were on to the social worker—in the past we have been asking for their help, now they are asking, they are at the limits of their coping.

> I am trying to think clearly.

> Now I know that Anna went to "panel" yesterday—that is, the social worker had put together an assessment for NHS continuing care. But it was thrown out, because she is under 65. She has to go to another panel.

> Early-onset dementia doesn't fit their categories, so Anna has a social worker from the older persons team—having been rejected by the adult team—and she is seen by an old-age

psychiatrist, but the assessment now has to be considered by the adult panel.

So her trial is set for two weeks ahead . . .

The blog does not fit easily into traditional categories—it could be like a letter to family or friend, but it is more public than that; it could be like a more formal publication, but it does not have to meet external criteria before it goes out. In this case it had both characteristics, first as a way of communicating with those close to me, a way of countering my own feelings of isolation and fear, and later—though this was not my intention at the time of writing it—providing the material for an article published in a professional journal, *Dementia* (T. Dartington, 2007)

Another extract:

"I can't cope," she says. I know how she feels . . . I think how my state of mind may be like hers. There are times that she also has to live with herself, hanging on until she recognizes someone or something. "I don't know you." She sees people she does not recognize. It makes her think that this is therefore not her house. There is logic to that.

I look at the blank puzzlement on Anna's face. With dementia it seems you get lost even in your own head. You don't even recognize your own thoughts.

I sense that there is a default survival mode, like a computer on standby—what I would call a gin and chocolate existence.[2] Thinking slows—my conversation is repetitive with Anna—full of ontological reassurance— "I'm here"—"Where are you?"— "I'm here"—"Yes?"—"Yes."

In this blog I explored the metamorphosis—an appropriately Kafkaesque concept—experienced by the family member in becoming what in bland social services jargon is called the carer. I experienced directly the mood swings between the heroic and the stoical. At times I saw myself as coping or non-coping with the stress of caring, and as being active or passive in relation to the challenges: on one axis, saint and sinner, and on the other, hero and martyr. As saint, I have a sense that I am doing the right thing; but as sinner, that I am not up to the challenge. As hero, I have a sense that I am making a difference; as martyr, though, I am resigned to my fate and very sorry for myself. We had visitors, good friends and family, as well as a growing queue of professionals. And the comments of others would reinforce these states of mind. "What you are doing is wonderful"—I was going on sainthood. "I can see you're stressed"—I experienced the stress as the wages of sin. "I admire your courage"—I was definitely heroic! "I don't know how you do it"—martyrdom awaits. I described this phenomenon in a contribution to a book that described carers' experiences, where the detail was different in each case but the overall themes of bewilderment, stress, anger, and a surprising element of joy were evident (Whitman, 2009).

I reflected afterwards: "I remember it all now as a kind of golden time. This must sound daft. But the uncertainties, the panics, the emergencies, were now under control, I felt, and we had a system that was rigorous enough to cope with whatever Anna's illness threw at us. And what I miss now is the sense of community that developed around Anna to counter the isolation of her illness" (Whitman, 2009, p. 194).

But there were problems along the way, and there still are, in putting these ideas together now. From my research, I knew that it is possible to be frightened of those who are vulnerable, as if we unconsciously expect them to attack us. This attempt at integration of the professional and the personal also draws attention to a very significant dynamic to do with societal values and family values in relation to the vulnerable. With two clinical professionals, a doctor and a nurse, I gave a case presentation at a prestigious research conference to do with palliative care, and the conference chairman thanked me and my colleagues very warmly and then—different from the other presentations—decided not to take any questions from the floor. What, then, was he afraid of? Some excess of emotionality, I suspect—and this fits with a hypothesis that the care relationship has to be carefully monitored so that it does not get out of control, in an excess of love or of hate, or both.

My hypothesis is that the professional leadership in health and social care is representative of wider societal values, as expressed then in the state provision of services, through the NHS in particular. So there is an emphasis on objective criteria of eligibility, the efficient management of finite resources, through the work of NICE, through the CSCI and its successor the Care Quality Commission (CQC), as well as political judgements about the prioritization of different services, as I have described in chapter twelve, on the costs of care.

There is a characteristic of dementia that is well known but is often not clearly formulated, and it has to do with dying. People with dementia may die of other conditions or of a mix of dementia and other conditions; or, in end-stage dementia, we may truly think that they die of the dementia itself—though coroners may not accept this. And even in hospital, there may be a reluctance to accept the inevitable, as the researcher in an NHS continuing-care ward found: "We don't like it when they die. We want to keep them alive until they are 100 or 101 like the Queen Mother" (Holman, 2006, p. 306). The illness is long-drawn-out—sometimes estimated, as a norm, as taking eight years from diagnosis. This is only a rough guide, as the illness will have been present before, undiagnosed perhaps for some years, and the progression of the disease is unpredictable. All of this leads us to a heightened awareness of the human condition, of the certainty of death but the uncertainty of its timing, the why and the when, but also—and this does not get the same attention—the how of dying.

There is an uncertain concept of a good death (Smith, 2000), and a study of palliative care illustrated well the uncertainties of an unplanned death, in the community or in a care home (Sampson et al., 2009):

> [District nurse:] "It is not easy to get a patient with dementia through the Continuing Care panel—it is difficult to know when they are at the end of life and it frequently comes as a shock when they die."

> [Care home staff:] "Those who you expect to return following an admission, do not and those you think you will not see again, come back."

We need an approach to palliative care that has a very much longer time frame than a few days or weeks.

This is the context in which I want to describe my experience of the community of care that came together around a person who was dying in her own home. This community was, as you might expect, multicultural. One of the most important carers had been coming to the house for years, as a cleaner. She lived locally, in north London, but came from a working-class community in the north-east of England. Her skills adapted well to the new situation, as she danced and read poetry with her former employer. Others were strangers to begin with and had to learn their way.

Their cultural differences could be observed in practice, with conflict around their interpretation of the task. The intractability of the care task—it would not go away, nor could it be resolved by any intervention—encouraged a defensive regression to difference, to allow the free expression of projective identification, reverting from depressive to paranoid-schizoid thinking.

A carer from Sierra Leone gave an account of the racism she had experienced in one placement: "She called me a nigger." We found that some carers were better than others, and most of the carers were black—but also from different countries, cultures, faiths. Criticism was difficult, and there was a lot that could not be said without first establishing a culture of trust.

As well as the cultural diversity, we had a mixed economy of care—involving family members, friends, volunteers, economic migrants from Eastern Europe, local authority workers, primary health workers (district nurses), dementia specialists, and psychiatrists. We were experiencing the globalization of care. A live-in carer was from Sierra Leone, as I said. While she was away, we also had two younger people: a Muslim from Kenya, training as a medical student in Turkey, and going to work in the United States, and paying for it all by working as a carer in the United Kingdom, and then, over Christmas, we had a Czech student, writing a dissertation on baptism for her philosophy and theology degree—and wanting to be a social worker. We were able to employ young women from Poland, recently admitted to the European Union. The carers from the local authority included a Scottish Catholic married to a Turk, and a Ugandan Asian, always elegant in her hajib. There was a volunteer, introduced by Age Concern, with startling died hair and tattoos, who also became a very good friend. Evening care was difficult at times, and we had three or four different people coming during the week. Even the best had to ask questions, which could cause frustration all round, and some others did not bother to ask, which was worse. Those that found it too difficult stopped coming. One Polish young woman kept on coming over three years. The carers from the different systems—from the agency who provided the live-in care, from the local authority, and those we employed directly—did not always get on, as I have indicated: sometimes there was a sullen stand-off or occasional shouting matches. Perhaps we should expect these tensions—the intransigence of the illness can make anyone defensive of their competence.

There were always going to be crises when any one of them was away for any reason, but, generally speaking, we had an effective palliative care system in place. So we had a quiet time over an Easter weekend. On Good Friday the young woman carer told me how on Saturday she and her boyfriend would go to the Polish church with their food in a basket to be blessed. The local authority evening carer did not come, but we coped somehow. On the news there was another teenage killing, a boy knifed in north London. The next evening the carer came in, looking, I thought, especially beautiful with her eyes made up—she had been that day to see the body of her nephew, the boy who had been knifed that I heard about on the television news. This was a dramatic expression of the breadth of the care economy, a process of extended reciprocal altruism, a dying person looked after by someone herself experiencing tragedy in the black-on-black crime culture of the inner city. In our London borough, like others, life expectancy from non-violent as well as violent causes varies dramatically along a single bus route.

What can we learn from this narrative of the dynamics of care and the interplay of cultural and task differences? This case study, if we can call it that, is illustrative of several themes that I had been researching over the years.

One theme is to do with the downwards force of delegation to do with physical care. For example, the opportunities now for nurses to do nursing are limited—delegated to relatively much less trained or less qualified care assistants. It is a process that in history and different cultures has been pervasive. It is the culture of the wet-nurse and the dalit, the "untouchable" in Indian society, where acts of care and compassion, from breast-feeding to the cleaning up of excrement, are delegated to the menial members of society—and, one may observe, even from outside of society, with the employment, for example, of "illegals" as household servants in the United States and the United Kingdom, or in contracted-out cleaning services for the NHS.

The professionalization of care leads inevitably to specialisms— a four-year nursing degree course leaves you overqualified to wipe bottoms. Social work is now more about care management than making dependable relationships. The GP, once known as the family doctor, may now see more patients in a well-appointed health centre, with time-limited consultations and extended hours, meeting QOF (Quality and Outcome Framework) targets, according to Department of Health priorities, but does not have time or motivation to make frequent home visits to the terminally ill. In many such ways, the heroic wins out over the stoical.

Cultural differences associated with gender and race, social class, and other factors to do with migrant status also serve to confirm this implied hierarchy in the management of care in intransigent circumstances of non-recovery. There is, in effect, a process of social institutionalization, not as obvious as in the old asylums but still insidious in its effects.

It is important to recognize and work with this societal dimension to the dynamics of fragmentation and integration. The care relationship—no doubt destructive when it goes wrong in a certain number of well-documented cases—is remarkable for its empathetic robustness and persistence against the odds, and this is not so well documented. The empathy and altruism that are necessary to carry out the task of meeting dependency needs in society are characteristic of family and of traditional community dynamics, but not so much, I have suggested, of the wider society. The state, being focused primarily on wider socio-economic interests—the greatest happiness of those with the greatest economic power—rather on than family or community interests, is neither altruistic not empathetic in the provision of resources to meet the needs of those who are most vulnerable in society. This creates a tension in the provision of services, and the necessary resources of empathy and altruism are accessed, as I have described, though the interplay of cultural and task factors in the day-to-day operation of systems of care, often in ways that are informal and deviant from a centrally generated audit culture of protocols and frameworks. Love—as well as guilt and reparation—and gratitude—as well as envy—are powerful drivers of human interaction, as we know from the work of Klein and others, and this psychoanalytic understanding draws our intention back to the underlying dynamics of care—below the radar of much of social policy and practice.

It is said that an ancient ascetic, seeing a starving tigress with her young cubs, threw himself off the cliff to be food for these animals. However extreme this sounds, it may remind us that it is not so unusual for people to sacrifice themselves for others. I did not understand how this works in practice until my wife had Alzheimer's. This was when I found that I was responding to her need, without consciously considering at the time whether I had a choice to do something else. I would have said, as husbands very often do, that I loved her. But now I reflect on what seemed to be an instinctual response to her dependency. I am saying this, not as an expression of emotion but as a very ordinary fact, not at all unusual, but so common that it mostly goes unremarked and unexamined. This quality of emotional commitment is not something I would attempt to describe or explain. It leads some towards and some against religion; it had me reading philosophers from the Stoics to Kierkegaard; it may be thought in psychoanalytic terms to be a move beyond narcissism to a level of emotional giving that is beyond concern, caring, or compassion (Symington, 1994). You see it in any number of partners, wives, husbands, daughters, sons as they look after the most basic and intimate needs of those who apparently have nothing to give back.

I used to think that there is no such thing as an altogether altruistic act, that you always get something back. I still think this is true, but I also am now aware that it is possible to act without the expectation of getting anything back—and that is what I am now calling altruism. There is much here still to explain. Our selfish genes seem to have lost the plot. If this is evolutionary psychology, I can only speculate that there was a time when it was not expedient to walk away from social responsibilities, that the need for group cohesion underpins family values, so that it is a matter of the greatest importance, of psychological survival as well as social cohesion, that there are discussions in countless homes whether the grandchildren will be going to visit Gran or Nan this Christmas.

There are also countervailing forces at work. I certainly did not love my wife all the time. I could be indifferent to her needs, and there are occasions when I felt a sudden blind rage, an anger of such intensity that I can say that I was experiencing hate, not love.

"You hate me," she said, and I of course had to deny it. The ancient Gods could love and hate like humans. It seems that we have to pretend differently, to pretend that we are made in the image of an all-loving God. There are very many human emotions that cannot be properly respected or expressed. Soldiers often find it difficult to talk about their experiences, except perhaps to other soldiers. They know that those without these experiences will not understand the complexity of their emotions, or the apparent incongruities of what their memories bring up for them. And there are many other less extreme circumstances where nevertheless "you had to be there". Caring for someone who is very ill is one of these. I am conscious that I write here as a man. Most accounts of the experience of caring are about and by women. When a male gets into this emotional no-man's-land, he may resort to a somewhat jocular humour, as in a book that I found helpful, *The Selfish Pig's Guide to Caring* (Marriott, 2003). I associate this with the "taboo on tenderness", which threatens to "lose the generosity of the child without acquiring the stability and integration which should belong to the adult" (Suttie, 1935).

If I want someone to understand the experience of being a carer, I refer them to Samuel Beckett, and his play *Endgame* (1958). According to his biographer, "Beckett characterised the general tenor of this play as one of 'extreme anxiety.' Hamm is afraid Clov might leave him. At the same time, he must be afraid that Clov will be able to find a life for himself outside the room, and also that Clov might find nothing but a terrible void" (Bair, 1978, p. 496).

So the person with Alzheimer's should not expect to get a loving response very much of the time, even in the most benign of circumstances. Apart from the mysteries of altruistic love, there is little to help even the most well-meaning of us from flinching at this image presented of the collapse of identity as ordinarily understood.

There is a well-worn joke about the distinguished visitor to a nursing home, saying, "Do you know who I am?" "No dear, but if you go to the office, I'm sure matron will tell you." The puzzled look of someone who cannot distinguish the familiar face of the other who has lived with them for forty years, or seems to think that her daughter is her mother, is a look that strips bare our emotional beliefs about self and other.

We are programmed generally—in evolutionary selection this must always have been a good skill to have—to be very good at recognizing faces. In early childhood we lose the capacity to distinguish the faces of animals with the same clarity, but we continue to build up a lifetime library of human mug shots—"I know the face." And then it can happen that sometimes we do not.

There is no point in visiting, we say: he does not know us any more. If the other person does not recognize us, we reason, it is as if we are not there. It is our sense of our own self that is affronted. And we act then as if the other has lost his identity, is not the person he was—a perception that is as true (or false) about ourselves as it is about him.

There are many other characteristics of Alzheimer's that are unusually threatening. In her description of the emotional as well as the physical deterioration associated with dementia, Rachael Davenhill (2007b) uses a telling phrase: "the ego is emptied out." This helps us to think how someone is no longer the person we knew. A psychoanalytically informed psychiatrist can also help in thinking about loss and depression, and about the defensive uses of forgetfulness as well as the realities of memory loss. "The catastrophically wounded ego of the patient protects itself by splitting and projecting rather than depressing and denying: a function that it is no longer capable of. Projective identification can also be a way of merely evacuating unwanted mental states" (Evans, 2008, p. 168).

Paul Terry (2006) has described how projective identification justifies the inadvertent neglect of older people—where fears of dependency, loneliness, and death are disowned and projected into the older person. He describes an observation of people with dementia and their interactions with carers and family visitors:

> They are painfully losing their independence and losing their mind. However the carers and the visiting wife contribute to these losses by infantilizing these old people. Treating them as children is projecting dependency into them and effectively stealing any remaining independent capacities for thought or action that these people may have left. [Terry, 2006, p. 6]

We all think we know about the process of ageing, but we do not want to see it fast-forwarded in someone we know. It is easier, therefore, to see Alzheimer's as something else, a mental break-down, or incipient blindness perhaps, something that can be understood, or where there can at least be the pretence of understanding. Professionals working closely with someone with dementia, using insights from Winnicott and others to do with the trauma of early childhood experience, have seen how, "as the capacity for words and the processing of thought diminishes, there is an increased reliance on the use of unconscious communications to convey experience" (Malloy, 2009, p. 119). An appearance of exaggerated senescence breaks a social taboo—worse than bringing attention to our inevitable and disgraceful record of morbidity by talking as we do to family and friends about our symptoms, the Alzheimer's person demonstrates the symptoms experientially. At a psychological level of experience, it is the mental equivalent of peeling back the skin and exposing the decomposition that is going on. This painful image illustrates the disgust that may be aroused by someone with Alzheimer's. Someone with dementia may become aggressive, even violent; may be forgetful, turning on water or gas taps, stumbling on stairs, or—an illustration quoted much more often than it happens in reality—wandering defencelessly down the street at night. This behaviour is properly frightening in its own right, and there has to be a response. But it also serves a useful social purpose: it gives us a good-enough reason to lock them up.

The person with Alzheimer's is bemused at all this activity. She lives in the present. Open up her brain, and the synapses would say *carpe diem*, seize the day. The ordinary awareness of time drops away, and the immediate is everything. All kinds of things seem fresh and new if your short-term memory is shot to pieces—and then seem fresh and new all over again.

Notes

The epigraph (p. 139) is reproduced from "Geriatric", by R. S. Thomas (2004), by permission of Bloodaxe Books.

1. This "panel" of commissioners and managers of services determines whether a service user is eligible for NHS continuing care. Continuing care is part of a free NHS; social care is means tested. At the time, I experienced the process as an anonymous Star Chamber.

2. For example, living on comfort foods.

CHAPTER FOURTEEN

My unfaithful brain:
a journey into Alzheimer's Disease

Anna Dartington (with Rebekah Pratt)

> The outsider is well placed to observe the world. The marginal
> position is a potentially creative one because the intellectual
> and emotional distance from familiar experience makes a space
> for a new viewpoint or an original thought to take shape.
>
> Anna Dartington

*Anna talked with a psychology student, Rebekah Pratt, as she came
to terms with her diagnosis of Alzheimer's Disease at the age of 54.
This chapter is an edited digest, taken from the transcripts of their
discussions over eight sessions. The final section is taken from further notes that I took of conversations with Anna.*

It comes up like the fox, very very quietly

Can I tell you about the day my brain left me? My unfaithful brain left me slowly, but there were also a few exact
moments that marked the start of when my brain began
to leave. I know I didn't lose my brain, but my brain lost me.
It lost me at a very important meeting for securing funding for
research, when all of a sudden there were no words. I couldn't

even say "I can't say anything"; is there anything worse than that? Maybe it left itself behind with my briefcase, full with a career built on thinking, and forgotten on an underground train. Could I have known then I was right on the cusp of moving from being somebody working well in the world to being someone who would soon not work at all? Maybe it was left with the newly begun doctoral research, now archived into boxes. It left me while playing Scrabble with my family, and it left me when I needed it to guide my coordination as I walked though the world as an independent, energetic woman with a successful career and busy life.

These moments came up on me like the fox, very, very quietly. It was these series of moments, taken together, that started to build into a sense of knowing that something was wrong. One of the first times I knew that these moments were more than a series of unrelated mishaps was on holiday. I went to paint the wonderful hibiscus flowers I look forward to seeing each year in the little part of Greece we travel to. I went to paint these flowers, but I couldn't do anything. I didn't realize till then how much that things were happening with my brain, that it wasn't working. This year we went on holiday and I saw these lovely flowers again. This time I didn't try to draw them; somebody else must do it now.

It was frightening to know things were changing, to know these series of moments were accumulating into an overall sense of something really being wrong. A friend who is a doctor eventually began to notice the changes that were happening. He intervened and encouraged me to have these changes investigated. It was one thing to know in private that my brain had become unfaithful, but it was frightening to learn that my brain's private betrayal had become publicly observable.

There is science, which has to be done,
but there also has to be compassion

Finding out what was causing my difficulties was explored in a lengthy diagnostic process. This marked the start of negotiating new relationships with professionals, where I was placed in the unfamiliar role of "the patient". My mother had a series of strokes not long before I started experiencing difficulties, and the initial investigations explored the impact of depression upon my memory and speech. Once depression was ruled out, more detailed assessments were carried out during a stay in hospital.

Hospital life required me to be the patient, and to act the way a patient has to be. I was constantly available for many tests, including taking blood daily. This not only hurt, but also left me feeling like an object, a real thing, a pin cushion. The hospital was a very large and frightening place. The staff were not very good at saying what they were doing and why they were doing it. I was frightened by the changes I was experiencing, and by the tests and scans, but in a way the staff seemed frightened too. Were they frightened at being confronted by a 54-year-old woman in the process of acquiring a diagnosis of Alzheimer's Disease, or was it to do with the sometimes fiercely hierarchical medical world they were working in? Whatever it was, there was a frightening feeling throughout the ward.

In this frightening environment people were held in the singular position of being constantly restricted to their beds. My experiences as a psychotherapist, social worker, and nurse left me feeling that holding people in such a physically immobile posture reinforced the idea of being a patient and of being ill. I desperately wanted to improve the setting and felt more could be done to encourage a feeling of wellness. The physical immobilization reflected a wider emotional immobilization, with patients—and even staff—being held in an emotional posture of fear.

Perhaps one of the most frightening things that happened during my time in hospital was having a brain biopsy. It was put to me that there would be better information about how things were through using the biopsy to look at part of my brain. When I think back I am not longer sure why I consented to the biopsy, or even whom I did it for. Did I do it for the doctors at the hospital? For science? For me? For something? If I could make that decision again, I would probably make a different decision. Should consent for such a procedure be asked for when someone is in such a frightened position?

Some of the staff did provide compassion alongside medicine. Compassion came in small gestures. One of the doctors always made a point of sitting by me, perhaps because I was the youngest person in the ward. I found this gesture very thoughtful, providing some acknowledgement of how I was as an individual. Even when going through a difficult time, compassion can be given through the way people speak and interact with you.

An explanation of my diagnosis of Alzheimer's Disease was eventually shared with me by a young registrar. This nice young man showed me the pictures of my brain captured on the scans, explaining the dots and markings that showed the difference between what my brain should be like and what it had become. Even though I didn't always understand it, it was important for me to try to understand what was happening and what my diagnosis was. Ultimately I needed to know the truth about what was happening to me so I would know what I had to work with.

The busybodies and the mediators

The diagnosis of Alzheimer's Disease brought many changes into my life, and one of those changes was starting to have new professionals enter my life. I had been entered into a system where I receive home-care visits on a daily basis from a range of carers who provide assistance with a range of daily tasks. For me it was difficult to be put into this system of care, and it is one I didn't really want to be taking part in. I have gone along with it, but it is not something that I wanted. I wanted just to be left by myself, but, along with Alzheimer's Disease, some decisions have become no longer about my needs alone. My husband wants to know I'm alright after he goes to work. We all have our worries, and when we have different concerns it's not easy, but he worries about the way I am, and this is why the carers come.

I don't mind having someone help me, although I can still do most things on my own. Sometimes I feel that there are others who might need carers more than me. I have noticed that despite my initial objections to this system, there are times when I don't mind the carer coming, and there are times when I find the carer very difficult. The difference in the experience of the carer is connected to a number of things, but in particular some carers give the impression of being busybodies, whereas others can act as mediators who work with me to negotiate this new reality.

The busybodies leave me feeling taken down a peg. Sometimes this is because the carer is a young woman who tells me what to do. I may indeed be difficult for these carers as I can do most things, and they are focused on completing a set of tasks through instruction. I feel put down, having these people younger than me telling me what to do. When you are capable of finding your own clothes, it is very difficult to be asked "Where are your socks?" The busybodies rush through in a hurry, disrupting my desire to start my day at my own pace. Having the carers come was something I would not choose, and the busybodies reinforce the sense that my choices are becoming less my own. I don't want to be case-worked. I want to just look out of the window if I want to.

Not only is having a busybody carer hard for me, but it is hard for the carer too. Being a busybody can define the relationship between the carer and the person receiving the care. When a carer starts pushing me around, I don't like it. The extent of our relationship is, "No thanks, I can do it myself." When I think about the relationships I had with people I worked with, I knew those people and, in comparison, I don't know these people at all. If I said to one of those girls, "What is it like for you?" she would just say "What?" They don't want me to talk to them. I suppose somehow I actually feel insulted by it all. They talk to me like a child, and I don't like it. Some people even act as if I might be contagious, a thing to be handled carefully with rubber gloves.

I have a very different experience with the carers who are mediators. The mediators work with me in negotiating the world on my own terms. The carers find different ways in which to build a relationship with me so that this can happen; with one it is the reassurance of a friendly smile, while another uses humour. Finding a way to communicate makes the way for the relationship in which we can work together to do what needs to be done. With one carer we share a joke, in that I will call her "mother" as she comes to help me along. We can share a joke like this because this carer is confident in her own authority, does not compromise my own ability to make decisions, and is caring. Sharing a joke together lightens the situation for me—and for her, as being a carer can be a difficult job.

I was thought of as a mediator in my own professional life for the adolescents I worked with, but it does not mean I know what it takes to be a mediator. It may have been easier for me to be a mediator in that I only worked with people who chose to come to me, whereas I have not chosen to have these carers working with me. One possible difference between the busybodies and the mediators is being able to have empathy. To be able to mediate, you need both to know what it might be like for another person and to have an emotional connection to your job. To have empathy for those you work with means being able to consider their experience. Perhaps the busybodies find it difficult to confront the issues of change and loss when thinking about what Alzheimer's Disease might be like for others.

I've lost so much of my autonomy

I had a career that was reliant on language, and now my language is starting to fail me. I will be in the middle of talking, knowing exactly what I want to say, and end up babbling. One of the most terrible things is just my brain saying "I'm doing something else", and this is what I feel is happening when my words fail me. That's the main thing in some ways; once you have lost your words, there's nothing. You can say, right I'm in control of this—but you are not. It is like losing autonomy over yourself when you lose your words. I have lost the autonomy that the full command over language can give.

In my working life I had a lot of autonomy and independence, and this loss of autonomy has spread through different dimensions of my life. The loss of autonomy started with the time I spent in hospital being assessed, feeling like I was redefined as a patient and confined to my bed. Since that time, my loss of autonomy is illustrated by the things I can no longer do, the things I need to ask for help with, and my changing abilities. In this sense, the carers that visit can represent the help I would like to not need. When they help with things I can do alone, it can be an affront to my continued efforts to maintain as much of my autonomy as I can.

Autonomy in my relationship with others has also changed. I now rely on my husband to act as an extension for my own memory and thinking. This means that there are times when he makes decisions that I do not necessarily agree with, despite the overwhelming support and strength he has shown. The fact I now rely on others, be it he or one of the carers who visit, to facilitate the expression of my autonomy is a compromise in itself, compared to the independence I am used to. My husband and I are now also known as the "carer and patient", which is a new title for us. Sometimes it is as if my diagnosis has merged us into a new singular unit. We now work more as a team, and he lets me use him as an extension of my memory.

You have to be able to bear the sorrow

Facing change is hard, particularly the changes that come with a progressive illness like Alzheimer's Disease. There are a number of things I have lost that have caused me great sadness. The first of these was stopping my work, and stopping my doctoral research. It was hard to give up something that meant so much, and it continues to be hard to accept the loss of some of my own abilities. I know that words are becoming harder to find and string together into the sentences I want to use to express myself. I am finding that there are times when my thoughts work better and times when they are slower. It is becoming more difficult to speak when I am trying to express myself quickly, as well as when I am trying to talk about issues of emotional significance for me. I also know my perception has been affected by Alzheimer's Disease, causing me difficulties with vision.

It has taken time to find a way to approach abilities that are declining. My instinct is to hold on to things that are becoming difficult to do, because I might never have that particular ability again. But then, on the other side, it is sometimes so hard to hold on, and it is so easy to leave it. Somewhere in the middle there is a balance in holding on to abilities while it is productive, but also knowing when to let go. I had wanted to learn how to play the piano, but as with so many new activities, to attempt them is to risk not being able to bear the potential sorrow that will come should I not be able to succeed.

The Alzheimer's outsider

> We are all fundamentally alone with our own experience and at the same time, willingly or unwillingly, but inevitably, an integral part of human groups: at work, in families, as citizens and members of the wider society.
>
> Anna Dartington (1994), p. 91

To have Alzheimer's is to be on the outside of wider society. This happens in many different ways. For me, the first move to the outer edges was leaving the world of work prematurely. The world of work provided such a concrete daily reality, and to leave it unexpectedly was a difficult adjustment.

Relationships with other people highlight the outsider aspect of Alzheimer's Disease. In relation to professionals we now have contact with, there is a sense of no longer trusting me to remember important things. Carers will speak to my husband as if I am not there, in order to pass on information. At one psychiatric appointment the psychiatrist asked me, do you know why you are here? I said, Yes, I've got Alzheimer's. He then asked me what I thought that to mean, and I described how there are tangles in your brain. He then put me outside in a chair—like this little Milly Molly Mandy—so he could speak to my husband. Even though he also spent time with me alone, I felt relegated to the outside of this exchange. I have even become an outsider to discussions about me.

Sometimes you are placed on the outside when others with no knowledge of Alzheimer's Disease try to understand your difficulties. For example, my walking has been affected, and if I happen to stumble some people think I have been drinking. If I need to take a seat, or rest, people cannot see my disability and may interpret my behaviour as pushiness or being lazy. Sometimes my difficulties are pointed out by others to my husband, as if I am not there. My age may compound this sense of being an outsider, as many people's experience of Alzheimer's Disease is that of older people—fathers, mothers, uncles, aunts—and not that of wives, husbands, sisters, brothers.

Something that reinforces the idea of being an outsider is when people only visit me in pairs, as if they are worried that something may happen or go wrong during a visit. People often visit only if my husband is also there, as if my individuality has been redefined into a comfortable pair, and this makes me feel terrible. Sometimes there is a sense that people are waiting for your demise. There are only windows into knowing what others think of the experience of Alzheimer's Disease and how it may have changed my life. These windows give a sense of me being an outsider in relation to wider society.

The now, the then, and the in-between

It has been a great disappointment to have this sort of stop in a sort of halfway life. I think, I feel, I wish I could have had the whole world, my whole brain, and I wish I could have used it more, so I was, in a way, stopped from something I was doing. I'm not bitter, but I realize it could just have been easier. Some of the things that have happened to me in my life might make other people feel sorry for me, and I wouldn't particularly want that to happen. In a way I'm becoming more secretive now; otherwise I might have to tell people about my lost abilities or that I feel I didn't finish something in my life.

When I think about the future, I think mostly about dying. In a way, when I think about dying, it is as if it is just something that happens. The only thing to think about it is how it is going to happen, and all I can do is say that I want my husband to be with me and I want to be at home. We have sorted out as much as we can really. I am adamant that I want to die at home and not in hospital, in so much as that can be; there is no reason why that shouldn't happen. I have a feeling that I will know that I am going to die before it happens. I've always expected that I would get quite a lot of headaches before something happens; that's just because I feel it in me, nobody's told me that. Once I had a friend who was helping me but she had to go home; my husband was out and I was on my own, and I started feeling like my head was a bit funny, that I had a headache. Even though I know I am not close to dying, headaches trigger feelings of fear about dying alone. On that day when I was on my own, I felt an overwhelming sense of being alone and even of being abandoned, and that I may never see people, like my friend who had had to leave, ever again.

Between now and death there is the in-between, and while I'm okay now, I don't know for how much longer. I plan to carry on and try to have as much fun as I can. We have holidays to take in our special place in Greece. I want to have loveliness, all sorts of cakes and fine things. I have gained a deeper appreciation for the fine things in life, for flowers, the arrangement of colours, and humour. I think about writing poetry and am trying to find a way to do this, most likely with my husband's help. I also spend time feeling sad, and sometimes I think about death. I work with a psychoanalyst to reflect on the feelings I have and the changes I am experiencing.

I think that when I first knew I had Alzheimer's, I was probably struggling with it. I think the difference now is that I know I can still do things. You could certainly say I've grown up. Before I was busy being clever and planning to do things, but then this struck me. I have had to learn to be patient and to let myself just be. This isn't always easy for me, but I am trying to just go with it. Despite the challenges of Alzheimer's Disease, my daily life continues in some very usual and familiar ways. I think, laugh, talk, garden; we have visitors; we travel. In many ways, life continues as it always has. While I have lost some things from my life, I retain much and plan to continue making the most of that.

I spend time reflecting on metaphor as a way of exploring my experiences and feelings. I saw a stem of flowers that reminded me of how it feels to have Alzheimer's. The stem had interesting leaves that looked a little foreboding and a subtle beautiful flower at the tip of the stem. When the flowers are nearly indistinguishable from the leaves, it reminds me of something I feel when people come and see me. Sometimes I know they know I have this thing and sometimes they don't, and I think that's how I feel: I'm a bit of this and a bit of that. I really can sit down and talk, and I also get terribly tired. I wonder if others can distinguish the leaves from the flower when they spend time with me.

I know my story hasn't finished yet. I may now need someone to work with me, to make another voice for me, so I can continue to tell my story. Working together with someone, I can tell my story in a way in which I can still be in it. Together we have told this story, and it worked, it worked really well.

Managing frustration

This section continues in Anna's own words, as I made a note of them at the time.

I just try and work it out really, there isn't much I can do, except to have these pills that I have, that I think are magic and are actually keeping me alive.

There was an odd thing that happened yesterday. It was like I described before, when the fox comes quietly.

When I was in the supermarket, what you were saying to me wasn't what I saw. Suddenly there was something I could not do, I could not have, I could not get then—a special washing liquid for my clothes.

This is the killer, where everything gets scrabbled—funny, I was playing scrabble when I lost it before. It was like that this morning again. I cannot even remember it now. It may be twisted—or it may be a good insight. I think you have seen both of those.

My eyes are a part of it. They are good. But people have not seen what I have seen. You are being the scribe of that.

It is always something down to earth. I was thinking, we had gone to the supermarket, which we did—I wanted the purple washing liquid they have there. I thought I heard you say it was not there. This is the desiccated brain. It is difficult to describe. The ordinary brain is easy to understand.

It is awful for you to think about it. You said the man over the road would have it. I did not understand.

It is possible—this is my good brain thinking—that this means something. I have had a good brain: it does come forth sometimes. Can we describe this to our friends, when we see them again?

Out there I was thinking about the purple washing liquid. It is not madness. It is confusion. It could go into madness. I hope it will not. When I am mad, I know I am mad. The thing that turned in my brain was that we went to that place (the supermarket) and we did not get the thing (the washing liquid).

The actual thing that we were party to, that got in my hair, the only good that it can bring is that if we explain, some people could understand it.

I remember being in the hospital the first time, feeling like this, dreamy, worrying what was going to happen. This is the other side of what we are saying. Why can it not all be put together? Why can we not go to the supermarket now and get what we want? It is a real mix-up. Even you get mixed up.

I got in a muddle about the supermarket like the hospital, not liking the place, about the things that I cannot have . . . if we are going to be interpretative about myself. I could see in the hospital people struggling with their words, trying to get out of the prison.

I like going to the sea. I will not be like this then.

Was I in a fugue? If I said that, I was getting uppity. But it probably is what we are talking about. You are talking to somebody and you cannot connect. In a fugue, you are trying to get rid of something frightening. We want to get to the edge of talking about it, and this will be part of the book, I hope. It is not bad to jump into the madness if you can get out of it. But it is frightening, and I do not want to get further into it. I am trying to get the other things in perspective.

Some people would like to dissect all of this. But these are ordinary things. We did not have a row. You got my new glasses. The changing of the glasses has something to do with it. I wanted the new glasses desperately, and when I got them I was changed a bit. This is an odd way of talking. Others would think I was mad, but it gives an insight into what it is like. I have the insight because I have been through it. I cannot stand up and talk like before, but I think it is worth describing.

Let's get back into the world.

Note

This chapter is adapted from A. Dartington (with R. Pratt), "My Unfaithful Brain", in R. Davenhill (Ed.), *Looking into Later Life: A Psychoanalytic Approach to Depression and Dementia in Old Age*. London: Karnac, 2007.

CHAPTER FIFTEEN

Learning to live with dementia

Who can tell me who I am?

King Lear

This chapter is an account I put together later from notes and diary entries to describe a day in our lives, in December 2002, when Anna was becoming increasingly dependent in the mild-to-moderate stage of Alzheimer's Disease.

8.00 am. No rushing today. I'm not going anywhere. Anna has a pained-looking face: she has had another bad night, crying. "I don't know why. It's all about fertility, growing things." I make a coffee for Anna, and she goes for her bath. I open an email from an old friend. He says: "I feel as though for some time I haven't really had a clear understanding of how your lives work in this circumstance." I am thinking how to respond to this, when Anna calls out that my bath is ready. This is my cue to go and help her to dress.

Underwear is full of openings: knickers have three, tops have four. If you can't see the difference, you have a 2:1 or 3:1 possibility of getting it wrong. And then there is the question of back-to-front and inside-out. The odds against getting it right double and double again and become overwhelming. Sometimes Anna and I fight over her clothes like we are wrestling. When I wash her hair, she says I am a good daddy.

We asked for advice from the specialist cognitive disorders people at the hospital, and were told that Anna has "visuo-perceptual and visuo-spatial deficits". So that explains it.

Anna has dislodged the bath plug but there is still some foamy water and I top it up with hot. I lie in the bath and read the sports pages. Anna comes in to tell me she is worried about a shelf in the kitchen. Her project day by day is to make her environment less confusing. When she is not worrying about the shelf, she is worrying about the garden, where there used to be a pond to catch the reflection of the moon. I say we can plant a bush or I can fill it in.

Anna sees me emptying the pond, but now has not remembered our conversation and protests that I should not do anything in the garden without talking to her about it. It often happens that she says, I wish you'd told me, after a conversation that she has forgotten. I explain, repeating myself, and hearing my voice take on a corrosive coating of reasonableness.

The garden used to be quite overgrown, which had its problems but it was private. Over the year Anna has cut away all the brambles and creepers, an old and twisted vine by the kitchen door, and exposed a weak and battered fence, which hardly has the strength to stand up by itself. Every day when she can she is out there with secateurs, as if she is cutting away at the tangles in her brain.

An hour has gone already and I don't seem to have had any time. I phone the number of a psychologist, but she is busy with a client. I don't know if she will be able to help, as hers is an old-age psychiatry service and Anna is under 60. And I don't know what Anna would think about this, but a social worker had suggested I make the contact.

I have her purple pen on my desk and she takes it back. "Never say you're sorry," she says.

I am trying to think of three things at the same time. Anna suddenly says, "I have a feeling that the people next door have gone." What? What did you say?

As she goes, she says, "Every day something frightening happens." Paranoia is a terrible waste of time.

1.00 pm.   I start to make lunch. I am cutting up some leeks, when Anna says: "I used to do that. Why don't you ask me?" I leave it to her, but she has difficulty holding the knife.

In the early afternoon there are old classics on the television. This is a time of low energy in our house, as Margaret Lockwood vibrates as the Wicked Lady or Gary Cooper gets tense to breaking point in *High Noon*. Anna is interested in none of this, nor in *Teletubbies*—notoriously the favourite of Iris Murdoch in the late stages of Alzheimer's.

Anna talks of getting the *Iris* video, which came out in 2002. Sometimes I write down what she says. "I don't want to frighten people." But she also says: "I can't do anything clever any more."

What does it mean to say, she is not the person she was?

John Clare wrote a poem, "I Am", in the 1840s, long before his death in Northampton Asylum:

I am—yet what I am none cares or knows,
My friends forsake me like a memory lost;
I am the self-consumer of my woes . . . [in Bate, 2004]

In that sense, we are all on our own. The philosophers say that there is no arguing with the statement, I am. Thank God for that.

We can observe pain in others—also their thoughts, if we observe a pained expression. On holiday in Greece, some years ago, after I had been bitten by a stone fish, a lady approached Anna on the beach—"Excuse me," she said politely, "But I could not help observing that your husband is in agony." She suggested peeing on my foot, but fortunately there was also a doctor on the island to give me cortisone. But the outsider's awareness is different from first-person awareness of pain.

John Locke (1690) described the person as capable of reason and reflection, the same thinker in a different time and place. David Hume, in his *A Treatise of Human Nature* (1740), described the person as a bundle of perceptions, bound together by causal connections. Are we Lockean persons or animals with Humean minds?

Dementia involves an intensification of moods. It involves recourse to ritual, confrontation, reconciliation, mutual adjustment, and development. I think Anna and I have been doing all of those things. This is a continental philosophical view, so I am told. Heidegger (1927) and his followers argued that we understand the world through our moods, and they emphasized how we experience the world through play and ritual. I learned about this because I went to a meeting of the philosophy interest group of the Royal College of Psychiatrists; the conference was titled "Dementia: Mind, Meaning and the Person" (Hughes, Louw, & Sabat, 2006).

I went to the conference as the guest of a psychiatrist friend. Three years before he had been the first to give us the beginning of a diagnosis, after we stayed with him and his wife, and they noticed how Anna got lost in their house and found it difficult to walk down their garden steps. He advised us to go to a neurologist, who was as reluctant as Anna's colleagues at work to see that anything was seriously wrong. It is as if those who should know are as scared of giving the diagnosis as anyone might be of getting it.

Then one day, in a psychologist's office, Anna could not fit the arms and legs to the torso on a doll, and she did not recognize the picture of an elephant. I asked the psychologist what this meant. She said nothing but silently passed me a leaflet for the Alzheimer's Society. I remember how cold she was and how cold I felt. The diagnostic process went on relentlessly for more than a year from that moment, until they had exhausted all possibilities and a brain biopsy had confirmed what everyone already knew.

Anna sleeps in the afternoon. "Sometimes I get so tired, when I shut my eyes I could just die."

A psychoanalyst, Valerie Sinason, wrote a poem after seeing a man with Alzheimer's. She described the condition as "a daily funeral" (Sinason, 1992). Juvenal, in his satire on old age, wrote: "And yet, worse than any physical loss is the mental decay which cannot remember servants' names, nor the face of the friend with whom he dined the previous evening, nor even the children, his very own, whom he raised himself" (Juvenal, 1992).

After the terrors of diagnosis, Anna has had the benefit of donepezil (Aracept). I heard at the conference that some people become so aware of their condition that they are suicidal and are then taken off the medication. I don't agree with that. I argue for insight, whatever the cost.

My GP prescribed me fluoxetine (Prozac). Like the lady on the beach, she saw I was in distress. It worked well enough. I became very calm in a crisis, which is no bad thing. I was going to an important work meeting, was caught in a traffic pile-up, was seriously late and did not break into a sweat, walked in, and began in my own time. But I could not always be in the slow lane. I stopped taking the drug, though I took the risk that I would be going too fast for Anna.

We say of people with dementia that they are no longer the person they once were. But none of us are. We may, however, want to think that there is a core self that is not negotiable. Merleau-Ponty talks of experience that has become sedimented (Matthews, 2002). For example, a dementing person may keep a sense of the importance of politeness in social relations, or may remember the conventions of previous relatedness.

According to this argument, there can be a strengthening of a sense of selfhood if the surroundings are right. I am beginning to think that philosophers are more helpful than psychologists in the situation that we are in.

What am I to think when a doctor describes treating Alzheimer's patients as like doing vetinerary medicine? One of our cats climbs onto my knee and then onto the keyboard of the computer. He was shot by some anonymous neighbours with an air pellet, and it cost us an arm and a leg—but not his, fortunately—to keep him alive.

Research observation of people with dementia is that they have "a rigid set of social standards" or are not wanting to be touched. This sounds normal to me. I am beginning to realize that Alzheimer's is not just a neurological but a social disease in a post-dependency culture, where good-enough parenting and containment is not understood or valued.

The anthropologist Mary Douglas (1966) has observed that it is only in the West that we are so cautious in associating animal characteristics with human nature. In other cultures, animal spirits are very definitely alive and well in the human psyche. If we had more of that culture, we would not be so fearful of what we don't understand or call less than human someone who is self-evidently one of us. Dementia makes philosophers of us all, and when not much is happening, everything is interesting.

6.00 pm.   The early evening is always a difficult time. We have a certain ritual then, a time for confrontation and reconciliation, watching the television news. Anna has a glass of white wine, a Grenache that she has become attached to and we order by the case. I drink whisky, Bells, from the corner shop—"the boys", we call them, as we make a gentle stroll most days for a top-up of washing-up liquid, fruit juice, custard desserts. A slow slug of alcohol works as a reward and a prop.

The violence in the news is hard for Anna to take. "Why are they attacking Iraq? The Americans don't own the oil. I can't bear it." And Israel. Anna remembers visiting Israel, when she was working on a conference there. "Bethlehem was closed. How can they do that?" Around the time of the Cuba missile crisis, I had a girlfriend at university who used to cry openly at the news.

What was the experience of Job?

> I was not in safety, neither had I rest, neither was I quiet; yet trouble came. [Job, 3:26]

On holiday Anna and I would play Scrabble at this time in the evening. Then she could not do it. The last time, on a Greek island, we tried again. I worked out a way of playing, where together we would look at both sets of letters and decide what to play. We stopped after the first three moves.

B
P L E A D
T
T
E X I T
R

Not unnaturally, Anna lost interest in the game and this scarily un-conscious message, as if we were staring at a kind of ouija board. Is there such a thing as a good death, when the traveller has to cross the Styx without a mind? She must be able to recall at least one story to amuse the Harpies—Harry Cayton, Chief Executive of the Alzheimer's Society, had said that at the philosophy conference.

9.30 pm. Anna is in bed. I am filling in a form, a Caregivers Diary, which I picked up at the conference. It is designed to be a help to carers who don't know Anna. The information won't do any harm, I think, but they are on their own with their instincts, mostly. Dressing. I tick the box: "needs some help". Add the info: "wait till she asks for help". It sounds so simple.

We are getting used to living with form-filling. We have to apply every six months for the Disability Living Allowance, as if a remission or recovery were a possibility. It is bad enough living with a degenerative disease without keeping on entering details of the wasting-away of ordinary competence.

We know very well the Mini-Mental State Examination. Anna had an argument with the doctor about what was the season. She did not like to think it was winter. She could name common objects and even spell "world" backwards—relevant, perhaps, as so much of her life is back to front. She is good at saying, "no if ands or buts", but there is no way she could draw a five-sided figure or keep on subtracting 7 from a 100. She will just have to get by without those skills.

Twice she was put through a three-hour battery of tests. She was asked her definition of words. She knew very well that winter was the cold season, and that to repair was to make better, to put together what was in pieces. Asked about fabric, she talked of society, fabric, of what holds society together. The psychologist scored her for accuracy, not the interest she had in ideas of reparation, of community. What is a sentence? "A group of words that make sense, with a verb. It is a group of words . . ." She wanted to go on to talk about words that give atmosphere: "no," she says, "not atmosphere but meaning," but the psychologist had ticked the box and was moving on. Consume? Anna: "eat, more than that, break down substances as in fire, complete destruction."

Enough of that, no need to get passionate. The young psychologist doing her research degree asks next, "What is the meaning of regulation?" Anna: "the attempt to make things work together, in the human body, in politics, wherever you have to stand in line, when you don't want to."

Question: terminate? (Does she know what she is asking?) Anna responds. "The end. Make it finish." Would that she could. This is the professional version of *The Weakest Link*.

Anna continues to answer correctly—Q. commence? A. "start."

Q. domestic? A. "to do with household " Q. tranquil A. "very calm"—these are the easy questions in the quiz.

The final questions reveal more of Anna's mind. Sanctuary? "A place to go to think and be alone." Compassion, she says, is "kindness, thoughtfulness about other people, identifying with their lot, helping them."

Parameter? "Outer boundary." This is from someone who knows also about inner boundaries, about the fragmentation of the ego.

To encumber? "To make life difficult for you, by giving you too much to think about or carry. You're going to be frustrated at the time."

Indeed she was, but Anna did well in that first phase. The next questions invited her to give her views on a number of matters, like a bizarre market-research interview.

Why do we wash clothes? "If not, they would fall to pieces." Why do we cook food? "To seal it against germs, and so that it taste better." What about the employment of children? "They would get too tired, get ill, we have to protect them, not exploit them."

Why register a marriage? "So no one runs off with the money."

That reminds me that I must call the solicitor. We have to protect our assets. Anna's mother sits in a nursing home on the hill. She is 92, vulnerable after a series of strokes. The capital from selling her retirement flat is almost gone, and she lives alone in her head. Anna visits and strokes her hand. She has power of attorney for her mother, though she herself can hardly sign her name to the cheques.

In the tests, it was the drawings that did for Anna. "I was never very good at drawing", she said.

Seneca was the tutor to Nero, not that it did him much good. The emperor, having murdered his wife and mother and brother, and many more, sent orders that Seneca should kill himself. As Seneca said, not to be surprised, no one was unaware that Nero was cruel. He cut his veins but the blood did not flow fast enough; he drank hemlock, but that did not work. He sank in a vapour bath "where he suffocated to death slowly, in torment but with equanimity, undisturbed by the disturbances of fortune." I learn these facts from reading *The Consolations of Philosophy*, by Alain de Botton (2000). And I have always found the misfortunes of others consoling. Everyone I know has their own tragedy. Our situation is both unique and hopelessly familiar.

"What? Neither gone nor dead?"—Hamm, speaking in *Endgame* (Beckett, 1958).

Every day we get mail offering to lend money from all kinds of banks and credit companies. We won't borrow because we have no prospect of paying back debts. I watch the news, and the Chancellor of the Exchequer announces a doubling of the government borrowing. They say they are taking the hard decisions, being prudent. What do they know? The pundits are shouting over each other. They all seem to have selective memories, but I don't think there will be more money for people with Alzheimer's in our society.

We get the odd gift. I was invited to the Social Services office, where I was given £150 in a brown envelope, "to spend on yourself". The only stipulation was that I was not to spend it on care for Anna. Later I got an invitation for carers to a weekend in a Holiday Inn in the Midlands. Now Anna has received a computer printout from the Department of Work and Pensions. "We will pay £10.00 into your bank account or building society account. This is your Christmas bonus for 2002." The letter then goes into a long explanation that she is eligible for only one £10 bonus and if she gets another by mistake she should contact her local Social Security office and hand herself in.

A quarter after midnight. On an impulse I phone my sister, in Canada, five hours behind. They live in an isolated farm in Ontario, and tonight they have eight inches of snow and a temperature of 20 degrees Fahrenheit. As I said, we all have problems. We talk for nearly an hour—there is no censorious two-second glitch in the interchanges, something to do with what is now digital that was then analogue, no doubt, and fibre optics, so that we can communicate without effort, while in our own brains the neurones are beginning to struggle to keep up.

The efficiency of the technology does not compensate for the loss of dead parents.

Before going to bed, I clean my teeth. The hot tap is running, must have been running for hours. I think of my father, how he turned off lights when we were still sitting there, and I wonder how he would have coped with the small-scale extravagances of dementia.

Anna is disturbed as I get into bed: "Who was coming up the stairs?" I ask: "Can I help you?" She is puzzled: "You are not Marks & Spencer." We settle down. "You are not my husband. Only in a soap."

Note

This chapter and chapter seventeen are adapted from my paper, "Two Days in December", *Dementia*, Vol. 6, No. 3 (2007), pp. 327–341.

Two weeks in 2006

I'll go no more a-roving.

Lord Byron

This chapter is drawn from a blog that I wrote over a six-month period. These were the first entries that I made, in May 2006, as I tried to make sense of what was happening to Anna and myself.

Sunday, May 14

I don't know how you do it, people say.

Nor do I. It is worth thinking about, what you learn from living with someone with dementia, about them, about yourself, about how we think about a lot of things in this hypercognitive world.

Anna is saying something. I've missed it. I say, Yes, and she looks at me, knowing I haven't been listening. "What did I say?" I don't know and she can't remember. She gets up out of her chair. She walks to the front door. I guide her back into the room, try to offer her a drink, get her to sit down. "I'm cold," she says. I put her shawl around her. The heating is already on, we are doing our bit for global warming.

"I want to . . ." She can't complete the sentence and looks at me, begging me to understand. She wants to go to—the toilet? Venice? Or any place in between. She is angry with me for not knowing.

It is a different world, where the wheels turn very very slowly. It costs me £10 a time to come out of this world—to pay for someone to be with Anna, to mediate, because on her own she cannot understand what is going on around her. I think of this tenner as a kind of toll I pay for living in the ordinary world. I am living with dementia, but so is she—all of the time. No ten-pound voucher for her to join the people she used to know.

I would like to think from the inside about living with dementia—what would help people living so far on the inside that you don't even know they are there—where they are faced all the time with the transience of things, when a thought is forgotten before it can be expressed. It's not all bad, that's the first thing to say. You focus on the essentials. It is not at all like meditation or other spiritual exercises. But you learn how to focus minutely on one thing at a time. There is no time to do anything else.

I look at Anna and she looks at me. She smiles. I smile. It is not always so peaceful, but for a moment we don't have to think about anything else. I try to imagine what it all looks like from her perspective. The blur of movement. The cacophony of sound. Meaning slipping away like a vivid dream you think you will remember but a moment later you don't.

She says, "Can I go with you?" I shake my head. "You don't want to go there," I say. But she would, of course, still, even as she stops on the threshold, paralysed with fear.

Monday, May 15

Of course Anna does not always smile. Suddenly she is angry and frightened—very difficult to find out why or what. Any help you give her is a threat—so that she rejects it all. "I can do it myself." But she can't do anything.

It is a dilemma, when you think someone is disturbed, you know they are, but you want still to respect their autonomy. Anna used to have quite a benign hallucination, that she was carrying one of the cats. She would clasp her arms round her bosom and seem very content and totally convinced by this. It did not seem necessary or helpful to say, there is no cat there; it made no sense to her.

But what if she wakes in the night, scared, pointing wildly in a sudden terror? You try to reassure, say there is nothing there. But this makes no sense to her, also.

The rules are different at home than they are in a consulting room—but there is the same need to hold a line, when it seems that reality is under threat.

The response is immediate. "You hate me". I make reassuring noises, less and less convincing with each repetition. "You're mad", she says. Or: "You think I'm mad." Whichever, it is a recognition that we are in different worlds at the moment. I am surprisingly calm, too calm. It is over six years since the diagnosis. I used to get more upset than this. Every change in Anna felt like there was a step missing and we were falling into hell. Worst were the psychological tests that recorded clinically her loss of spatial awareness, her losing the ability to recognize objects. But I am not shocked any more by the deterioration in her condition.

I despair at the way time is drained from each day, as we sit and stand, stand and sit, circle restlessly.

It may be she has an infection. It would be good if there is something we can do to help.

Tuesday, May 16

"He is too old for me." This was the reassuring comment that the carer made to Anna. It is a difficult thought, but Anna the jealous wife is wary of the women who have come into our life. Sometimes she thinks that all women must be after me—no cheap jokes, please—or more painfully that I will be after them, as she senses the loss of her own capacity to flirt, to charm, to seduce. (Though she has very successfully used that charm to get doctors and other professionals to listen to her, even now. As the psychiatrist, a woman, said to her recently, you have style.)

But sexuality is still an issue, as she struggles to hold on to her place in the world. There are two young carers, Polish, who sit with Anna some mornings and afternoons. They have a special patience and respect with Anna, which means that they are good at the job. They need this patience because often she will look angry when she first sees them, ask what they are doing in her house, and may be restless for an hour before she relaxes with them.

It was on one of these times yesterday that the young Polish carer said that I am too old for her. It will be all right as long as we can be light-hearted about these things, for the passions below are very real. "You want to leave. You hate me." No amount of reassurance takes away the fear.

Wednesday, May 17

It is a simple thing, I was going to have a drink with a friend, but I didn't make it. Anna had been complaining of headaches and her back and might have an infection and I could not think of anyone to come and be with her for a couple of hours. The care system was exhausted. Not much in itself, but it felt like a defeat. A door banging shut.

I get the support I can—including a weekly meeting with a psychoanalyst—but this week the carer on Wednesday mornings has gone home to Poland to celebrate her marriage, and there is not anyone else I can trust at this time. It is only the second time I have missed a session in six years, but it is the second time in six weeks. Another door bangs.

Thursday, May 18

I am in a state of mind when I am losing things. Put down my glasses and I don't find them again. I am having to use Anna's. Yesterday I was going to a meeting with social services and health about the support we are getting. I could not find a form, outlining the "care plan". I searched for two hours but I still can't find it, staring me in the face probably. Perhaps I can't bear to look at it.

At work, if I lost an important document like that, I would be worried. We talk about losing our mind. Anna wrote about how her unfaithful brain left her, as she said. "Maybe it left itself behind with my briefcase, full of a career built on thinking, and forgotten on an underground train."

I have a simple theory about losing things, that it happens when your mind has had enough. I remember some years ago getting up very early in the morning to go to an important meeting outside London. I had everything ready and went to go out the front door. No car keys. I looked, at first urgently and then with increasing panic, trying to remember where I might have put them down, what clothes I had been wearing, and so on. Finally I ran off down the road to catch a bus to the station—I arrived at my meeting, two minutes late. When I got home that evening, I found the keys: they were on a hook by the front door, exactly where they should have been. I reflected on this madness and thought that if I was that agitated it was better that I did not drive. Who knows, I might have had an accident. The failure of my mind may have saved me that day.

But the failure of Anna's mind—what is that saving her? She goes round in circles, literally, round and round the room, trying to complete a thought. "It's all from the garden." She means she had not liked a vegetarian dish the carer had prepared. That we can understand, but now she is struggling with something else: "You know, we were talking about it!" We were talking about all kinds of things, clothes, friends. I make a guess, I make a list of guesses. Her frustration is acute. "You know, you know!" But I don't. The thought is lost without a thinker.

Saturday, May 20

"I don't want to upset people." Anna used to say that, when she was still able to write her account of the illness. Why not? I thought. There has been a lot on television recently, including on *Coronation Street*. In the Alzheimer's Society newsletter the chief executive Neil Hunt commented that some people "think it focussed on the experience in such a negative way that it will deter people from seeking help. It is a difficult area. We know early diagnosis brings many benefits, but don't we have to face the fact that dementia does bring many desperate challenges?" I agree with him on that. The newsletter itself is—probably rightly—very positive in its approach, with success stories about self-help and support and tips for coping.

I remember when Anna and I were asked to a meeting with another couple. The woman—who had Alzheimer's—was silent, and the man spoke about her as if she was not there. I was able to observe how good Anna must have been as a family therapist, as she cut across the man and got the wife to speak for herself. At the end of the hour the man was distressed, his defences weakened. Was this helpful? I thought so at the time, though the professionals present looked uncomfortable. It was only when Anna was herself able to see a psychoanalyst that she found a professional who was able to talk about her fears about what was happening to her.

If we are not upsetting people, what are we doing? I see Anna's friends, when they visit, and how distressed they get. Dementia is upsetting in a particular way—it is devastating in its cruelty, as if we are being played with by a malignant spirit: so you thought you were clever, made in God's image, cock of the walk, king of the castle, the ego centre of your universe, well, we'll see about that. (Yes, I know these images are male—dementia is an attack on potency. Perhaps that is why of Anna's old friends, it is more often the women than the men who are still able to visit.)

Anna doesn't remember the details now when she has been angry, difficult, shouting at the carers, refusing to be helped. There was a lot of that in the last week, perhaps because she had a headache, perhaps an infection. Although she doesn't remember it all, she sometimes apologizes, as if she is trying very hard to be good. When she herself is in tears, this is natural enough—normal, if such a word has any meaning. It is difficult enough without having to be cheerful all the time.

Monday, May 22

8.00 in the evening and Anna has gone to bed, a grandmotherly carer with her, and I am hoping she will sleep, as she is tired. The front-door bell. It is one of those young men, unemployed, with a tray of cleaning materials for sale—our cupboards are bulging with them. I point at the notice on our front door—DOOR TO DOOR SALES? PLEASE DON'T RING.

"Can you read," I say, for starters.

"Yes, I can, sir, and can I explain, people sometimes move away
..."

I interrupt. "The notice is for a reason. I am not just been unfriendly. I have an invalid here and I don't want unnecessary calls."

"I didn't know that . . ."

"I'm telling you."

"You're not listening to me. The reason I rang is that people sometimes move away . . ."

"You're not listening to me," I say.

"Why are you shouting at me. Can't you see it's making me worse."

"I can," I say, and close the door.

"Cunt," he says. "I'll send my friends round."

Fortunately Anna has not woken up. This is a meeting of different worlds—the angry disturbed young man, treading the streets, doing his best, I suppose, and the angry (disturbed?) old man, trying to protect his home as a sanctuary of a kind. I complain about social isolation but I still want to protect the boundary if I can. And it is strange to build a defensive wall with vulnerable people on both sides.

We had a sociable weekend, more than usual, family and friends. Anna slept well and likes company, though she got lost in the conversation when there were more than two people. So, after lunch, she and I sat quietly together while the others finished the meal. She looked very sad, and I asked her what she was thinking. "I want to get out of it," she said. Meaning the illness, as if she could get out of a bad situation. Like I dreamed last night of getting out of a bad situation at work. You can always do that, walk away or get the sack. Isn't there an issue about prison sentences, that there has to be the possibility of remission even to life sentences to give the prisoner hope? In some cancers and MS and other diseases, there may be times of remission. I don't know if it is better or worse to be allowed hope and then have it taken away again. But it means that you can fight the inevitable.

I am not emotionally interested at all in the possibility of a cure for dementia. That sort of hope is not relevant for us. But we need to have some sense of progress (apart from the disease "progressing"), of making sense, of overcoming some problem or other set up by the fates.

In Philip Roth's new novel, *Everyman* (2006), his daughter repeats at his grave his stoical maxim, "There's no remaking reality. Just take it as it comes. Hold your ground and take it as it comes" (page 5; I have only been able to read a few pages as yet).

When I talk about the fates, does that mean anything other than reality? So I get exaggerated pleasure out of very small triumphs—repainting the hall is progress of a kind. Building a ramp into the garden will be a major achievement, even though we won't know until it's done if Anna will want to walk down it. A threshold can be as much an obstacle for her as a brick wall.

Tuesday, May 23

Do I think it's cathartic, writing this? I realize I take the question as a criticism. The *OED* definition of cathartic is of a purgative, "Producing the second grade of purgation, of which laxative is the first and drastic is the third." I don't know. Is that what I am wanting? I feel like I am writing messages in bottles and throwing them into the ether. It is difficult to write about experience. Soldiers don't talk about important stuff except to other veterans. You don't want the response, it must have been awful, I don't know how you survive, but that is the universal response.

I don't want to be going to the toilet in public, like Diogenes living in his tub in Athens. But I don't like the implication that living with dementia is somehow dirty, shameful, not something you talk about in polite society.

Of course, there is another question—do I want people I meet in other circumstances to know about this? Probably not. It is not relevant, and so probably they won't be interested to read this, even if they know about it. I have a simple observation that you don't have to scratch far below the surface to find a sorrowful story or two in almost anyone's life.

"I won't be a person who's horrible, bashing people about."

"I'm worried that it's going to go down. I'm usually quite white, upper."

In these ways Anna talks about her depression and the anger, both of which she wants to manage still. Her language is original but logical—it is common enough to talk of black moods but not of being white (e.g., cheerful).

She cannot manage her moods, of course, or her behaviour all of the time. In this she is like anyone else. She does not remember the details of her outbursts, but she remembers having them.

A week ago I went to a funeral, of a lovely old lady who had become a bit confused herself. I did not take Anna because of the crowds, an impressive send-off for an 85-year-old. I have just got a letter from her husband, who describes their last meeting, last summer, how Anna got to her feet and moved towards her and stood by her, as his wife sat, interested, attracted, warmed towards her, something mutual.

I have wondered about the friendships that could develop. Perhaps that is what day centres are for: Anna certainly was interested in one or two of the clients, the few times she attended. But I think a day centre is too groupish to allow real friendships easily. I have in mind very small clusters, perhaps two or three people living locally, sharing a support group perhaps. It would not be easy. There was a neighbour, who wanted to be a volunteer, who came to see us a couple of times, brought her knitting. But Anna turned against her, when I was away, and we lost her.

Wednesday, May 24

"I know now I'll never go away."

I was sitting with Anna after breakfast and she was distressed. "We can go places," I said.

"You can. I can't."

And then she asked again: "What is so awful about that place?" She was talking about Greece, I know. It was easy for me to guess that. And I explained again about the difficulty we would have in travelling there. She obviously thought I was not trying hard enough: "You're a big man." Yes, and if I could carry her, I would.

But she was not impressed. "I'll find someone to go with me. I'll have to find somebody else." It is as if I have failed her as a husband.

But then her independence left her. "I'll go to the toilet—[pause]—I don't know how to do it."

Later she was angry again. "You hate me, don't you." I offered her something for her headache. "You just want to get me out of it."

Then she tried to explain about something really good. She stood and waved her arms . . . "Green things, up there." I could not understand and she got more angry at my stupidity. She gestured about something that went round and round. I tried to find out if she was talking about food or clothes, or flowers in the garden, perhaps the rose bushes.

"Don't do this to me." She was really frustrated now. She explained again: "Boys like it." Her arms waving again, she gripped my hand with sudden force. "It's up there." Eventually—and this was after an hour or more—I thought she said, lights? and I guessed, Christmas trees, and that was right, I think. Anna looked relieved and became calm, though by then I don't think she remembered what she had started out to explain. And why she would talk about a Christmas tree at the beginning of summer I was not to know.

I am of the generation that read R. D. Laing in the 1960s. Laing listened to the sense of what people said and took what they said seriously, even though they had a diagnosis of schizophrenia and were talking like they were quite mad. How to listen to someone with dementia? The sense is there, but the associations are wild and the gaps between the words get wider and wider.

There is someone—I forget the name, anyone know?—who has written poetry from conversations with people with dementia. Psychoanalysts and others listen to the music behind the words. In Tavistock group relations conferences, some people do well with understanding what is going on, when they are unfamiliar with the language being spoken.

If I had thought of a Christmas tree earlier, it would have saved an hour of mental pain. This is more difficult than Sudoku. "It gets to my top," she said, meaning her headache. "I'm frightened I'll have no brain or something."

Friday, May 26

I was idly searching the internet for stuff written on Alzheimer's and found this in a research abstract: the sequence of deficit acquisition was heterogeneous. Meaning that everybody is different. And they can't predict and you never know quite what is going to happen next. They could have written much the same about Anna. "Impairment of semantic memory, visuo-spatial and attentional abilities eventually developed but the sequence of deficit acquisition was heterogeneous." Absolutely.

So we have something here that is progressive, irreversible, but also erratic. A good candidate for using the perspective of complexity theory: the individual like any system in a state of bounded instability on the edge of chaos. Sometimes it seems that it takes less than the beat of a butterfly's wing to change Anna's mood.

In a fast-moving world measured in nanoseconds, it is difficult to plan at any time. The instantly changing world of mobile phones for the many and BlackBerries for the few has made a virtue of living in the moment. Dementia is about living in the moment, but for different reasons—because of the difficulty of accessing information.

How do we plan for a disease like this? Six years after the diagnosis, eight years after we started to notice that something was going wrong, and years before that, if we had known, when there were processes getting under way to break up the connective patterns of Anna's brain, and yet still we find it difficult to have a coherent plan.

My brother says that we are playing catch up, and he is right. We make changes to the house, as Anna experiences a new difficulty. But we don't seem to be able to run ahead and make the changes ready for her.

The help we have received from the occupational therapists making their assessments has been pathetic, to be honest. But there are reasons for this. First, they have a disability model, which is helpful to some extent, but it is inflexible: it does not take into account that this disability is fluid, on the move all the time, will be different from the time of referral to the time of assessment to the time of introducing new aids. This is a professional rigidity that does not work with dementia. Second, there is a systemic rigidity, so that the referral process itself is linear, where one and one only response is allowed for any given stimulus, and then the case is closed.

Anne the carer is upstairs with Anna in the bathroom. She is brilliantly pragmatic, and as long as Anna can still use the old bath, they are holding on to her sense of her old identity and independence. "I don't need any help" is her cry of freedom. A wheelchair is under wraps under the stairs. Anna is virtually housebound, but she does not want to be an invalid.

I am learning about her increasing difficulty with crossing thresholds. I knew she was uncertain with steps and ledges, seemingly lacking the sense of perspective that can distinguish a flat surface from a cliff. So we have put in rails and have ramps on order. But the difficulty is not physical—she can walk as well as you and me. The problem is psychological and neurological and the threshold feels unsafe to her, even the flat floor going from the hall into the dining room, where she may stop for several minutes at a time, sliding her foot forward and back, unable to be reassured that she is safe.

So we continue to improvise, taking our lead from her. It is no good our having ideas if they don't work for her. My brother will build a wooden ramp, and we hope that Anna will soon feel safe to go into the garden again—it is looking good for her.

Saturday, May 27

I can hear Anna arguing upstairs with the carer. She does not recognize her, she says. It is the bank holiday weekend and half-term, and her usual carer is away. We have three regular carers, but the fourth carer who comes to cover for them has a difficult time. There are two or three who do this; they know Anna, but she does not know them.

Holidays are always disruptive. I used to make a joke about that, that holidays are a bad idea because they make people dissatisfied with the rest of their lives. Better to live all your life as if you are on holiday. Now we talk of continuity and consistency for Anna, but even when it is going very well there have to be disruptions to the routine. And she likes treats. Today we are driving to the country to see a friend.

I can feel the tension in me, hoping that we will have a good day. Anna is refusing to let the carer help her. I have to decide whether it will make it better or worse if I intervene.

"They hate me," Anna says. I try to reassure her and go back downstairs. I can hear some cries—could be Anna or the children next door, getting up.

The lunch goes a treat. There is a moment of sudden sadness, as Anna objects to a question our friend asks about my work. She feels left out, left behind again. "You're retired, you've done your bit," we say cheerily, insensitively, as she goes deep into what she has lost. The moment passes, and Anna is enjoying her beef and pasta. And I take pleasure in manipulating two forks alternately, so that she keeps eating. An example of a small triumph, rewarded with a smile.

Back home, in the evening, Anna again cannot make sense of the help she is getting from the carer. She feels that she is being assaulted by a stranger, and for two hours we talk about nothing else.

I think of T. S. Eliot and the women who come and go, talking of Michelangelo (Eliot, 1917).

There are times when I think that having a carer is a lot more trouble than not.

CHAPTER SEVENTEEN

The realities of care

Sometimes I think you've said goodbye
and now we're stranded speechless
on the platform, you on the train,
wishing the bloody thing would leave.

Barry Palmer

This chapter, again drawing on notes, diary entries, and now the blog, describes another day, four years after the account given in chapter fifteen. Anna was now in the severe stage of Alzheimer's Disease.

A day in December 2006

7.00 am.   I wake up much earlier these days, while it is still dark. And Anna seems to be sleeping later. I stretch my limbs carefully, aware of the increasing stiffening of the joints. I start to think of milestones. A lot of time has slipped away, and it is not easy to remember what we have lost. Even a few months ago Anna could do a lot more. We went on a picnic. We visited a friend. These things are not possible now.

I think, do I have time to go to the bathroom? We have a live-in carer now, and I can hear her moving around and I accept that today she has got to the bathroom first. For all the achievements that we make in our lives with such intellect and curiosity as we have, with our practical skills and our spirituality, in the end what matters in life is washing and toileting.

We have made some improvements to the bathroom, making more space and installing a walk in shower. Anna still does not like being helped with her personal care, but it is easier for the carers. Every morning I can hear her cries, but the panic is soon over. As a young carer said, "It is easier for us, we can be cruel." I know what she means, and she does not mean it badly. She can continue to work with Anna even when she is screaming. I do not tell her that I can also be cruel.

What she means is, being objective. I think of all the assessments that have been done, are still being done. Now, of course, I am also making my own observations. I can do my own review. Looking again—that's all review means. So I take note again of how Anna is frail, lost, how she looks like her mother, who died two years ago, aged 94. I look at Anna and see her mother's gleam, the eyes sharp out of a shrunken face. They were both tough ladies, and in their prime they fought like—cats? dogs?—like women of independent mind. I remember her mother well, and Anna is pleased when I talk about her. A Labour councillor of the old sort, she defended the rights of minorities until she became one herself. With Anna, I have the same sense of the power stripped off her, and all that is left is the residual authority in her eyes.

Anna is getting NHS care at last. In 1987 she went with her mother to the Labour Party celebrations of 40 years of the NHS. I remember Neil Kinnock singing. But her mother, a Labour stalwart for those forty years, with a signed photograph of Harold Wilson in her room, never got that NHS care in her nursing home: it was paid for by the sale of her house. Wilson retired early, though not as early as Anna. We learned much later that he also had Alzheimer's.

Six years into her diagnosis, Anna is still young to have dementia. I have heard that this may be to her advantage, that NHS per-capita budgeting limits are significantly higher if you are under 65. I'm sure they have a rationale for this, to do with their arcane calculations—like the QALY calculations about the cost effectiveness of drugs—about the value of a person's life. You should know that in the eyes of the state, you depreciate rapidly when you are past working age.

It is getting to 10.00 am, and Anna makes a very slow descent of the stairs. This is her work now.

She smiles when she hears my voice. Sight and sound have become split off from each other. She hardly recognizes objects at all now, but she does recognize sounds. And she is still sharp at recognizing how people are from their voice—how they are irritated or impatient, or relaxed with her.

But sometimes, if necessary, I am able to communicate with the carers about what to do by sign language, which Anna cannot see—behind her back, as it were, though I am standing in front of her. And when they sit with Anna, they watch television with the sound down. If it is a film, I put on the subtitles.

Anna does not know who is in the room, but she can hear voices in the next room, or even the family next door. She hears the cats mewing for food. She hears the police sirens in the main road. We put on meditative music. The music she used to like, Italian tenors, she finds too emotional.

She does not go in the garden now, and we bring flowers into the house. There is a fountain where the pond used to be and we have built a conservatory, but even that is difficult. There are ramps, but she does not like the wheelchair.

We have much more support now, which makes it easier. But this is because Anna is now very frail, which makes it more difficult. This is the homeostasis of decline. We have the live-in carer from an agency, paid for by the NHS. The social care she was needing for six years has reached a level where it is now reclassified as health. The social worker who had been our care manager for four years sent me an email: "I am writing to formally advise you of the new care arrangements . . ." Except that this has been confusing for us because health did not have any care managers to take over. And we continue to confuse the system, which cannot decide whether Anna is an older person because of her dementia or an adult (younger person) because of her age. I worry that the health and social welfare systems, oscillating wildly, could crash like my computer.

Almost no care is done by anyone who has grown up in our society—in London, anyway, that seems to be the case. It is shaming, I think.

"It was the best of times, it was the worst of times"—it is traditional to quote Dickens at Christmas time. Well, it was like that for us this Christmas. I chose a tree that was the same height as Anna. When I brought it into the house, I found that she could not recognize it. If she does not recognize visitors, she can respond to their voices, but not to a tree. A couple of her visitors before Christmas were in tears, and at times she would be crying too.

We are still eating Christmas cake but I can't keep any food past its best-by date. The carer, coming back after Christmas, has thrown away a whole round ripe Stilton—"It was smelling," she said. She is very careful about hygiene. She makes bland food for Anna and spiced chicken for herself and offers me some.

When she first arrived, two months ago, she came to us as mysterious as any stranger. We met at the underground station, and she was standing with her two suitcases, like the opening line in a short story. We knew nothing about each other, and in the few minutes driving her home I told her a little about Anna. "Oh, she has challenging behaviour!" She looked disconcerted at that, and I wondered what the agency had told her.

11.am. The carer sits in the corner of the living room, looking sideways at the silent television. I do that sometimes, but I don't like seeing others—seeing the boredom on her face. When she first arrived I asked if she had any questions. Yes, she said: How did she change the programmes on the television?

After lunch, I walk into the living room. Anna is standing in tears. The carer is brushing up crumbs from under her chair. But it is not her job to love Anna, except, I suppose, to love her neighbour as herself. The love of Anna is really my job, so I give Anna a hug.

Anna: "If she's going to be like that, I can't bear it. I was trying to get Tim because . . ." She does not finish. The sentence.

Then I have had to fetch the carer out of the kitchen to help Anna to the toilet. Anna says that she feels she is being told off, and I know what she means. There is no medication, the carer says. I find it for her. There is no bread, she says. I buy it. The shower is broken! I mend it. One of the cats has brought in a dead rat. I dispose of it.

She is good in lots of ways. She washes the floor. She washes clothes. I don't know if the washing machine will become exhausted. It is not an industrial model, for constant use. When I visited a residential home for the elderly, it seemed to have been designed to function as a laundry with bedrooms. The machines there were always breaking down under the strain.

Why, when we have a carer living in now, does Anna immediately look so much more like someone in an institution? Because she is so much frailer—the reason we need the care?

She stays at home because that is where we can be sure of her humanity. I read in the newspaper about Dr Alzheimer's first patient, a woman in her 50s (just like Anna then), who was so restless and confused that her doctors prescribed warm baths and, when that didn't work, chloroform. A hundred years on, a journalist describes the illness succinctly: "It strips people of their memory, their personality, and eventually their humanity."[1] Anna has certainly lost most of her memory. Her personality? All right, I am worrying about that, about her passivity at this time—but she only has to laugh and you know it is not all lost. She laughed on Christmas Day, as she mimicked acutely the Queen in her broadcast—to the gob-smacked admiration of the family who were present. But her humanity? Why is that on the list? She has not lost her humanity. What would that mean? What are the clinical signs of loss of humanity?

There are social signs of loss of humanity—for example, bad old stories of back wards in institutions of demented patients left to stink in their own urine and excrement. We hope we would not tolerate that now. But meanwhile anti-dementia drugs are not good value in the NHS, it has been decided, whereas antipsychotic drugs are, it seems—this is the progress, apparently, that we have made in a hundred years from warm baths, and if they don't work, give them chloroform. A social model of dementia ought by now to help us to distinguish what is to do with the disease and what is to do with social responses to the disease: see Tom Kitwood, who wrote

Dementia Reconsidered (1977)—some people must be reading him as his book was reprinted in 1998 (twice), 1999, 2000, 2001, 2002, 2003, 2004 (twice), 2005, 2006, etc.

I have been reading more philosophy since that conference in 2002 (see chapter fifteen), and more psychology, more humanity.

Alan Bennett wrote about his mother's depression:

> Nothing excuses us from the obligation to divert our fellow creatures. We must not be boring. And since for the specialist most illnesses soon cease to intrigue, if you have to suffer choose a condition that is rare. Should you want to catch the doctor's eye, the trick is to not to see no light at the end of the tunnel; anybody can do that. Rather mistake your wife for a hat and the doctor will never be away from your bedside. [Bennett, 2005, p. 34]

I remember a neurological professor who was very interested in Anna while there was a possibility she had anything but Alzheimer's. With the diagnosis confirmed, he lost scientific interest. Early-onset dementia made her interesting in a way, and unusual, but with each year passing even that originality is blunted.

I worry now that we are boring. That this is boring. Who would want to know about the everyday life of demented folk? Remember *Mrs Dale's Diary*? "I'm worried about Jim." Anna cries out to be ordinary—she does not want the drama of losing her mind.

6.00 pm.   Anna does not drink wine any more, or watch the news. I sit with her, saying nothing.

Am I a hostage? I think that sometimes, when I am alone with Anna. When I am alone with a thought that wants to be outside, making connections, leading to actions, but I am here inside, unable to move or make a connection. I think about Brian Keenan and the other hostages in Lebanon twenty years ago. I think of the years out of their lives, when they survived by keeping their imaginations alive in the here-and-now of getting through the next moment. Keenan wrote: "Something in the human spirit seeks to overcome such oppression. There is always something in us that will not submit" (Keenan, 1992, p. 180). My situation is not at all comparable. Not at all. It's the sort of thing that your parents say: there's always someone worse off than yourself, much worse off, more than you can even imagine. And not one or two, but in their millions, where numbers become statistics only. On the news, Saddam is dead but, four years on, the situation in Iraq is worse than ever. I think of the tragic damage of our human nature, our energetic mobilization of hate and capacity for killing, the political cannibalism that feeds on invasion, exploitation, and anonymous death. Whereas here I am working with the inevitable facts of our human morbidity—simply, in our case, with the tangles in the brain that can drag a person down while she is still alive, and all you can do is sit still and watch.

As I watch the young carers, as they use their curiosity to relate very helpfully to Anna, I read the psychoanalyst Margot Waddell:

> Care of the very elderly, those so often lacking the capacity to speak, yet so intensely riven by extreme emotional states, requires a painful reversal of the original pattern of container/ contained (the young now struggling to offer states of reverie to the old). [Waddell, 2002, p. 249]

As I said, the carer now has the spare room, where I was sleeping before, and that is where we keep the philosophy books. I miss the comfortable bed. I feel dispossessed, not in the same way but in sympathy with the way that Anna has been dispossessed of her mind.

I used to think this was a large house, big enough for a family with two adolescents, when we moved in twenty years ago. But we have extended the bathroom, and this took out one small bedroom. Another bedroom is now an upstairs sitting room for Anna, when she cannot manage the stairs. There is the spare room, which is now for the carer. So I now have my bed downstairs. After the first three nights of this new arrangement, my back seized up and I could hardly pull myself upright.

Before we got even more adaptations into the house, Anna was falling out of bed. "I've never done that," she said, after doing it again. I put her to bed one evening, and the doorbell went—by the time I'd answered the door, there was a crash and she had fallen. I found her on the floor again the next morning, looking more puzzled than hurt. I am able to lift her, but other carers are not permitted to do that. Health and Safety: it's what makes a home a Home.

Each time, she is confused and afraid again about where she is, when she is at home in bed.

"We'll go to our house? Yes? How can I get there? What are they doing? What has happened to me? What happened?"

"You are in bed now . . ."

"Oh good."

Bedtime is both wonderful and fraught. I remember—two months ago—settling Anna down on my own one evening:

"Is this a hospital here?"

I am reassuring. "It's your own bed. Warm, comfortable."

"Yes, if it is that. So this is home?"

Then she adds: "Obviously, if we can."

She is astute, this demented person. She has just summarized the issues we are working with, testing the combined talents and resources of the local authority and the primary care trust, and ourselves of course.

7.00 pm.   A second carer has arrived now to help Anna to bed. I hear Anna calling me, but I now leave them to it. At these times I suddenly feel very tired. I worry sometimes also that I may exclude the carer, treat her indifferently, as if her feelings don't matter. The different carers are sometimes very critical of each other, the morning carer critical of the evening carer, like the dynamic you might find with different shifts in residential care. She has not gone into residential care—but in a way she has.

It is past 8.00 pm and already Anna has fallen asleep. I am able to go out now, without having to think to arrange for someone to be with Anna. I can work when I like, the same as anyone. I can see friends, go and see a film. But I also have to get used to my diminished role in my own house, which has become somewhat of an institution, with me in the role of the janitor. I used to sit with Anna until she was sleeping. Now I must remember to put out the rubbish and lock the door.

Note

The epigraph (p. 215) is reproduced from "Stroke", by Barry Palmer (2002), by permission of John Koch of Annwn Books.

1. J. Lawrance: "It was discovered 100 years ago, but has the treatment of Alzheimer's progressed?" *The Independent*, 3 November 2006.

CHAPTER EIGHTEEN

Postscript—learning from experience

Life is full of surprises, mostly unpleasant.

W. R. Bion

This case study explores the understanding I gained, as a social scientist, in relation to the dynamics of care around vulnerable people, over the last six years of the progression of Anna's illness. In particular, I argued on her behalf for continuity and consistency in the visits of the local authority's home care team. I had the support of an Admiral Nurse (specialist in dementia care), who would discuss the possibility of residential care. I accepted this as likely, perhaps inevitable, not knowing exactly how the disease would progress, but I put forward as an organizing principle that if possible Anna should not have to leave our home while she was still able to understand and recognize where she was.

I would go and see the Admiral Nurse at the hospital. She might have visited me at home, but Anna could not understand why she was there, and it helped me to get a certain distance from the immediate situation. On one occasion I arrived at the hospital in such stress that her colleague thought that I was a patient waiting for a psychiatric appointment—an understandable mistake in the circumstances.

This is how the Admiral Nurse saw the situation:

"My initial focus was on supporting Tim in maintaining Anna's independence. As Anna's illness progressed my role changed to acknowledge Tim's feelings of grief and anger; feelings that re-emerged at times when Anna's needs increased or when the care package broke down. I worked with Tim to help channel his feelings into action.

A 'person-centred' approach was essential in meeting Anna's care needs. The occupational therapist coordinated a series of sessions for the formal and informal carers which we co-facilitated. These took the form of supervision, education, and support to help the carers reflect on situations and share experiences. Working together as a team was crucial to providing effective support to Anna."[1]

The occupational therapist was the most important of all the people who were giving us support. She was a continuous presence over the last four years—no arbitrary opening and closing of cases interrupted the continuity and consistency of her presence, and she was able to take a crucial reticulist or social-brokerage role:

"Over the four years I knew Anna, my role evolved: from occupational therapist to incorporation of the CPA [care programme approach] care coordinator and care manager roles. As an occupational therapist, I worked with Anna on her priorities, from finding practical solutions to personal care tasks through to sharing feelings related to having Alzheimer's.

As Anna's hold on herself and the world around her became more tenuous, the functioning of the complex care team became crucial. Connecting emotionally was inevitable: sadness, anger, doubts about competence and effectiveness, through to warmer feelings of concern abounded. Some of this could be understood as an unconscious communication from Anna about some of her experience of dementia. Members of the formal and informal network of carers needed support with these feelings too, if they were to be contained and cooperative working supported.

Longer term involvement meant I could act as a thread of continuity, keeping a hold of the many parts of a complex situation. This allowed for management of existing services and the timely introduction of new services as Anna's needs changed."[2]

Our experience was consistent with research that has subsequently been carried out on end-of-life care for people with dementia, which concluded: "With timely support in the community, it would be possible to prevent some crises occurring, or in the event of the crisis happening, provide an intervention that would reduce the need for a hospital admission" (Sampson et al., 2009).

Anna had severe visuo-spatial problems, so that simple tasks like climbing a step or picking up a glass became a challenge. The occupational therapist liaised with community occupational therapy services about aids and adaptations, as these became necessary. She also arranged for the speech therapist to visit and advise us on ways to overcome some of the communication difficulties that we had and, later, to help with feeding, as swallowing became more problematic. As staff on a hospital ward said, in the research study: "they have no message to their brain of hunger ... such a great help if carers are willing to help with feeding" (Sampson et al., 2009). At home it was possible to find individual ways of overcoming these difficulties.

Anna talked and laughed with friends and even in the late stages of dementia still recognized familiar voices, and impersonated the Queen's Speech at Christmas—but could not recognize the Christmas tree. She became unable to carry out any actions on her own, was disorientated and unable to follow any instructions, and in the end she was hardly able to communicate in an intelligible way. Her limbs were frequently in spasm, with involuntary movements. She was doubly incontinent. At times she would become agitated, and cry or hit out. The progress of the illness was monitored by the old-age psychiatrist, who was able to explain to me what was likely to happen next, although she was unable to give us a precise time frame.

"My initial contact with Anna and Tim involved monitoring her response to medication (donepezil and memantine). Unfortunately, she deteriorated rapidly, and the focus shifted to managing her agitation and distress. Her function declined and even simple tasks such as climbing the stairs became impossible.

The support of the community mental health team and in particular her occupational therapist and care manager was vital. We made numerous applications to social services to increase and adapt her care package as her needs changed.

Anna lost the ability to speak and express her wishes, but these changes had been discussed at an earlier stage. She became bedbound and then developed apnoeic episodes. At this stage we shifted focus towards avoiding acute hospital admission and fulfilling her wishes to die at home. We drafted an advance care plan—a new experience for an old-age psychiatrist—and the involvement of the palliative care team was instrumental in supporting this."[3]

The social care had increased according to Anna's increased dependency until there were four visits a day from the home care team, supported by up to four hours of informal carer visits. Anna was eventually thought to meet the criteria for NHS continuing care, and the care management passed to the primary care trust. This decision made possible the care in Anna's last nine months.

With the continuing advice of the social services care manager, we introduced a system of live-in care, while the existing care was maintained. Care in the family home was adapted to meet Anna's increasing need: at first handrails, then ramps for a wheelchair, then a hospital bed, a hoist, a shower chair. Unlike residential care, the care could be highly specific to Anna's needs. While she was still able to negotiate the stairs, she did so, however long it took.

This incremental approach meant that at this point the care exceeded ordinary expectations of what might be done at home. Each time the care was adjusted to accommodate a new crisis, the pressure to consider residential care or admission to hospital was reduced, until she was in the final stages of her illness.

In the research study, a GP said: "At the end someone panics and the patient is sent to hospital." And the outcome is predictable:

"Send an elderly patient with dementia to hospital and they will probably die. A&E is not the place for palliative dying patients" (Sampson et al., 2009).

On two successive Sundays—and therefore "out-of-hours"— Anna seemed to be in distress, having difficulty breathing. The emergency services were quick and efficient. On the first occasion, Anna was removed immediately to hospital, where the doctor in the A&E department proposed a series of investigative tests and was ready to admit Anna for observation. When he proposed inserting a catheter I was able to question the need for invasive treatment at this time, arguing successfully that continuing care at home was more appropriate. Otherwise, she might well have died then in hospital, or lingered on—a delayed-discharge statistic.

An ambulance manager, interviewed in the study, argued that a palliative care crisis intervention team was needed to prevent unnecessary end-of-life admissions (Sampson et al., 2009). On the second occasion that the emergency services were called, despite the sense of panic, I was able to argue at once against an immediate transfer to hospital, signing a disclaimer form for the paramedical services.

During the later stages of the illness, there were frequent review meetings, at which the care plan could be revised. The next review meeting was crucial. I drafted the content of the advance care plan—after the care manager explained what this was. It stated that the intention was to nurse Anna at home during the last stage of her illness. We made note of specific problems such as falls or pneumonia and the steps that would be taken to avoid emergency admission to hospital. The team had a new member: the palliative care consultant:

"Anna's wishes were well known and represented by Tim. She wanted to be cared for and to die at home. Her condition had deteriorated; she had experienced apnoeic attacks, which had frightened her carers, and she had narrowly avoided hospital admission. Carers needed confidence to manage her symptoms and permission not to call an ambulance.

The advance care plan was agreed at a case conference. Clear instructions were written and promulgated to all her carers explaining Anna's wishes and what to do if she had breathing difficulties or a fit. Carers also had contact numbers for advice or support.

District nursing and palliative care input was increased. Anna's GP prescribed oxygen and PRN [prescription required as needed] medication for symptoms that are common at the end of life, such as excess secretions. Out-of-hours services were informed of the plan."[4]

It was not necessary again to call on the emergency services for Anna. Oxygen and back-up medication were stored at the house. The psychiatrist was able to hold back from her professional impulse to arrange even now for hospital admission. The district nurse service was alerted and was on call from 8 am to midnight. (In fact, they were called only once, during an evening.) Anna's breathing continued to deteriorate, and she had difficulty swallowing. Diazepam was given when she became agitated. The psychiatrist and the palliative care consultant and her team also visited the home during the week that she died.

As Anna had said (chapter fourteen), "I am adamant that I want to die at home and not in hospital, in so much as that can be; there is no reason why that shouldn't happen."

Notes

This is an expanded version of my article, "Dying from Dementia—A Patient's Journey," *British Medical Journal*, Vol. 337 (2008), pp. 931–933.

1. Kate Coupe, Admiral Nurse, Barnet Enfield and Haringey Mental Health Trust, London N15 3TH.

2. Lynn Malloy, head occupational therapist, Barnet Enfield and Haringey Mental Health Trust, London N15 3TH.

3. Elizabeth L. Sampson, senior lecturer and honorary consultant in old-age psychiatry, Royal Free & University College Medical School, London NW3 2PF.

4. Mary Brennan, consultant in palliative care, North Middlesex University Hospital, London N18 1QX.

PART IV

CONCLUSIONS

CHAPTER NINETEEN

Reflections on partnership:
can we allow systems to care?

> The urge to make people happy is linked up with a strong
> feeling of responsibility and concern for them, which manifests
> itself in genuine sympathy with other people and in the ability
> to understand them, as they are and as they feel.
>
> Melanie Klein

What is to be learned and can be usefully applied from one family's experience? A personal account of organizing care around a vulnerable person living at home is not going to be fundamentally different from what others are doing, as they do what they can in a wide range of circumstances. In this final chapter, I would like to explore further whether it is really possible to plan for an integrative way of working that would meet the needs of vulnerable people for continuity and consistency in their care. Continuity and consistency are highlighted as needs that service users and carers have themselves emphasized (CSCI, 2005). Having described what I have in mind, I want then to look at the issues this raises in the real world of health and social care in the community.

I am arguing for a real integration of formal and informal systems of care—for example, by thinking of the delivery of care through very small networks equivalent to an extended kinship system. This idea comes out of the six years' close observation, as I have described, of the care of a person with early-onset dementia. By a process of trial and error, an effective support group came together around her care, as her needs increased. This support group included local authority home care workers, agency workers, untrained carers, a domestic cleaner who became a carer, and informal carers (family and friends); their work was given the necessary encouragement and support by a local authority social worker, by an occupational therapist from the CMHT (who organized meetings that included both formal and informal carers), and by their managers. They were all looking after other people as well. This ad hoc illustration of what works in practice provides a template for what might be planned and replicated around the needs of a vulnerable client. For example, it would be possible to think of a cluster of three or four clients, as I described in my blog (chapter sixteen), with the support of a home carers group. Such a group could work flexibly with the clients (and their family carers, where appropriate). If on one day a client were to be in particular distress, the care system would be able to respond immediately. However, if a client does not need so much support at a certain time—for example, during a family visit—this would release the care system to focus their energies elsewhere. They would provide services according to agreed care plans, but they would do so in a self-managing way, very much like informal carers.

This model would meet the need for continuity and consistency that clients are wanting—and which is difficult to provide through a conventional system, where carers are rotated on a daily or weekly basis by their managers. The group would be able to manage its own absences—holiday and sick leave, training days, and so on—and senior managers would only be involved where their system was showing signs of not being able to cope. Such a group of home carers might then be supported by a management team who would not be working in a directive way but working to maintain the capacity to be self-managing.

This is a simple illustration of a support system developed through a process of negotiating partnerships. (Isn't partnership always about negotiation? Up to a point: "We provide certain services, as laid down", "These are the hours we work", "These are the eligibility criteria we follow", "There are issues of patient confidentiality", etc.) It looks simple, but negotiating partnership arrangements tests the constraints of pre-existing system differences. A negotiated system is one where the partnership of different professionals arises naturally from a responsiveness to need. This happens, as I say, naturally, in all kinds of contexts, but it is not easily tolerated in current practice in the delivery of services, even those that are overtly patient-centred. Moreover, the partnership model would make little distinction between the formal and informal care being provided. As a recent study of the ethics of dementia care argued, "the appropriate attitude of professionals and care workers towards families should be that of partners in care, reflecting the solidarity being shown within the family" (Nuffield Council on Bioethics, 2009).

A difficulty with a negotiating partnership model is therefore that it is deviant according to command-and-control managerial structures and linear accountability systems. It follows a principle that *authority comes from the task*. In many aspects of our lives, we act responsively and do what has to be done. It should be possible to apply these principles to service delivery around vulnerable people.

I am reminded of the story of a consultant geriatrician who would take a screwdriver on domiciliary visits. An alternative might have been to refer to the occupational therapy service, who would arrange to make an assessment visit towards the end of a performance-monitored three-month waiting period, and then refer on in turn for a technician to make an appointment at a convenient time to fix a wonky table leg.

Perhaps I exaggerate to make a point. There are still carers who will say they do not do the washing-up or buy a loaf of bread, or who are told by their managers not to take their clients out into the garden, because the local authority would be liable if they have a fall. How do we avoid such aberrations and ensure that we allow for the kind of authority that comes from the task in a negotiating partnership model of care, without undermining the very necessary controls that have been established over time to protect vulnerable people from exploitation and abuse?

The negotiating partnership model provides the conditions for the effective use of resources according to need, with continuing review of good practice, while providing continuity and consistency of care and reducing social isolation. But at the same time we must recognize that it does not in itself protect against the possibility of inefficient use of limited resources, inequitable distribution of resources, the uncontrolled spread of self-serving restrictive practices disguised as good practices, and the unregulated abuse of vulnerable people—all the things that recent reforms in public services have been introduced to address.

We still have to put together the different views of human nature at work that Douglas McGregor (1960) described as Theory X and Theory Y. Treat people as immature and dependent, and they will respond accordingly. Treat them as responsible adults, and they are more likely to be so, but there are no guarantees. The challenge is to balance the right amount of direction with the optimum level of autonomy. You need controls and monitoring to ensure good performance, but you also have to authorize and acknowledge good performance as it happens spontaneously.

None of the basic assumptions famously identified by Wilfred Bion in his study of *Experiences in Groups* (1961)—an unconscious group identity momentarily built around the need for dependency, for fight–flight, or for pairing—is in itself unhelpful for a group working with the needs of vulnerable people. A work group may very well meet its unconsciously expressed needs and also do a good job.

However, those working in these contexts have been constrained by increasingly narrow definitions of task and a continuing separation of powers. In primary care, many general practices developed multidisciplinary teams of their own, only to be told that health visitors and district nurses could not attend their meetings: from a management perspective, this was considered a waste of time. Meanwhile the Department of Health tries yet again, with "integrated care pilots". A district nurse described giving a 90-year-old woman a bath in 1993, just as a new policy was coming in that district nurses should not be bathing patients: "Doing something as simple as giving someone a bath can make them feel so much better and have real heath benefits, so I just went ahead and did what I thought was best"[1] Sampson Low of UNISON, the trade union for care workers, has described how they are doing some of the work that district nurses used to do, but "the unofficial side of the social care job gets squeezed: it's difficult to do dignity in fifteen minutes".[2]

I have argued throughout for an operating principle where authority comes from the task. But what is the task? We need a system that allows for the expression of compassion. This implies a capacity to respond to the pain of another as if it is not another's (Feldman, 2005), and as such it is a capacity that is very efficient in family care. We have become so obsessed with monitoring efficiency in formal systems that belatedly there is a realization of the need to reintroduce compassion as a research project into nurse training (Davison & Williams, 2009). But compassion, like dignity, will not be achieved through targets. We have to think what would be the boundary conditions that would best allow for the expression of compassion, for protected spaces of local autonomy.

A process of negotiating partnership should allow for the development of appropriate boundaries. In our Tavistock research in a children's ward (Dartington, Henry, & Menzies Lyth, 1976; Menzies Lyth, 1973), the negotiated partnership included the families of the patients; nursery nurses, low in the hierarchy, were properly authorized to manage the care of the patient in relation to the family, standing in for the family only when necessary.

In the case study of Anna, an inside story of a pragmatic process of improvization across family and professional boundaries of a system of care, the negotiated partnership worked well when there was a space for local autonomy, and less well when those involved had to conform too closely to standard protocols. The story is unique, but not at all unusual. It is how things happen on the ground. It is messy, stressful, and unfair—because that is how life is. But it has the potential to achieve a quality of care that is responsive to need. Protocols attempt to meet need—which is not the same thing.

There is a certain hope that is now invested in the introduction of personalization of services. Professor Peter Beresford, an advocate for service users, has argued that direct payments and individual budgets, pioneered by the disabled people's movement, could become bureaucratic and inflexible and could undermine the NHS. "This raises the question of how we square the circle of a universalist NHS, still in many ways free at the point of delivery, with a model of cash payments or allowances borrowed from a selective social care system."[3] Personalization will be effective only if there is also attention to the underlying dynamics in the delivery of care. I have described some of these dynamics in the previous chapters. Until her last year, Anna was able to pay for her care from her NHS pension, so she had many of the freedoms of the personalization agenda. She attended a day centre for a few weeks, and while she was there she formed a relationship with a psychologist on secondment, and she made a presentation for the other clients on Florence Nightingale. But she stopped going when the staff saw her as only a client, not having something to contribute. At home she was able to have the treats that she liked: a visit to her favourite hairdresser, where she still bought her cosmetics; a visit from a young woman who gave her a massage. In such ordinary ways she retained her identity, while losing capacity. It would be good if such small freedoms were available to all and not means-tested in future proposals for the funding of social care. But however good the initiatives that are proposed, they will be subject to the same systemic constraints.

The experiences that I have described are not intended to be especially remarkable or revelatory. Such experiences lead to the sort of innovation that could be in the running for the annual Guardian Public Service Awards. In 2009 Sheffield city council's community services for older people won the transformation award for innovation and progress by focusing on a short-term intensive home-support programme: "Under the old system, the focus of home care was very task-orientated. Now the emphasis is on helping the person regain confidence and independence." At the same time there was to be long-term support for older people with mental health needs and for their carers. The service manager acknowledged that the transfer of some long-term support to independent agencies provoked anxiety among older people and their families.[4]

Good practices are relatively easy to introduce, but the organizational context in which initiatives flourish—or are constrained—are much more difficult to challenge or change. The local authority home care team who supported Anna over the years would not now be available to her. They are also now deployed on a more intensive programme, when people are in crisis, coming out of hospital, and so on, where the value for money and effectiveness of the services can be more easily assessed according to targets and outcomes, and the long haul of continuous care is entrusted to work of agencies. Of course, an agency worker may be quite as good (or indifferent) as a local authority worker, but, for example, from our experience, we were very aware of the effects of contractual differences, with agency workers arriving early or late, hurrying to finish their tasks to get on to the next job, while the local authority workers were more able to stay with Anna for the full thirty minutes or longer that had been assigned for their visit.

In earlier chapters I looked for an explanation of the powerful dynamic that separates out whole categories of care, at the macro-level of health and social care policy and the financing and management of services. At the most local level, as we have seen, the separation makes for very little sense and a lot of hardship. Those working around the vulnerable person are doing what they can to mitigate the effects of this separation of the heroic and the stoical in the interventions that they are making.

We may think about reparation and the delivery of services, that those who choose or find themselves in caring or therapeutic roles are motivated in part by an understandable internal need to make things better, to relieve suffering, to alleviate any distress in others, and that this is because of their own experience of distress in themselves and in others. Paul Hoggett has found that this kind of motivation is often put forward by those explaining why they entered careers in nursing, social welfare, medicine, and allied professions (Hoggett, Beedell, Juminez, Mayo, & Miller, 2006). If caring is to be seen as primarily a reparative task, and at an unconscious level that is always likely to be the case, then the rewards of caring can be very satisfying; conversely, though, if the rewards are not apparent, a sense of failure is felt to demonstrate inner deficiency and is intolerable (Roberts, 1994).

Such motivations are not easily expressed openly, and there may be a fear that they will be subjected to a cynical or contemptuous attack in a so-called me-society culture. Other motivations are, of course, also present at the same time and may have equal or greater weight: the need for recognition and status, for example, linked with societal anxiety and the desire for material wealth.

Where the reparative function within a system of care is damaged or disabled, then behaviours that are, on the face of it, benign and therapeutic are likely to become indifferent or even cruel in relation to the needs of a vulnerable client population. The reparative function is damaged where management systems are disrespectful of the motivation to "do the best we possibly can for our clients".[5] After all, who could argue against such a task? And yet care systems seem to find all kinds of ways that stop them doing the best for their clients.

Management practices that in themselves would seem to be necessary and reasonable may nevertheless be destructive of the reparative function if they are shifting the emphasis too much to an instrumental or survival-anxiety state-of-being. This shift serves a purpose. Make the relationship instrumental and it is more easily controlled—the attractive fantasy is that you can automatically make people more efficient, and so forth, through the use of protocols, "agenda for change", salary reviews, inspections, and audit. I have just been looking at a "Care Manager System" that promises over 1,400 pages of guidance, policies, and procedures, with a full instruction manual on how to run a quality care service, including over 200 (170 relating to community services) registration and regulation compliant policies and procedures and "providing your Care Business with everything you need to meet the CQC, RQIA, Care Commission/SCRC, CSSIW definition of quality assurance." This is a machine model of a system that works until it breaks down, a systems model that suits the political process, perhaps because politicians also would like to act as if they are omnipotent (they are "in power" until they are "out of power").

This approach also addresses a related anxiety that the autonomous worker, doing what he or she thinks is right, is out of control, like a loose ball bearing in the works. To the extent that this problem of out-of-control professional competence (and incompetence) has been successfully tackled (e.g., by general management in the NHS), we should expect to find a corresponding level of low morale—which is what has happened. The reparative aspect of the work has been diminished to the point that people say, "this is not what I entered the profession to do", while finding that they continue to be under attack as "forces of conservatism". Politicians, taking an instrumental view of wage rises for nurses, understandably feel misunderstood when they are slow-handclapped for their pains.

This argument has then to be put in a wider context. The question about the modernization of public services is not whether this is useful or destructive in this or that aspect—we can see that realistically it is a bit of both—but why it has been thought to be necessary for the survival of our economy. I suggest that there is a real fear that the needs of vulnerable people are so all-consuming that they threaten to be overwhelming to the rest of society. It is the threat that is hidden away in the Beatitudes, that the meek shall inherit the earth (not, as we have seen, that there is much evidence of that happening). It is the fear that every family experiences when the question arises, what do we do about mother/father, Uncle Bill, now that they are unable to look after themselves? It is the fear that, if we took their needs seriously, our own way of life would be seriously depleted. Macro-economists have argued whether the level of "generosity" in a benefit system affects adversely a country's economic performance, and welfare provision in industrialized societies has been put under severe pressure to meet competitive global demand (Glyn, 2006). The return to a fear about recession will not make governments more generous.

So the idea that has become a mantra—one not to be challenged but repeated at every opportunity—is that public services have to be as responsive to the need for change as any other enterprise in the global market. This is why business entrepreneurs are, de facto, thought to be good at running schools. Perhaps they are, if schools are to be thought of primarily as businesses working to achieve competitive advantage. We could as well argue that teachers also might in turn have something to offer to running businesses, if they were to bring their experience of working appropriately within a dependency culture into what is otherwise seen as a fight–flight economy, with its unforgiving need for successive short-term gains. Finally, a supermarket approach to quality is tough on suppliers, as we know, and in the end may offer the consumer limited choice. We may need to recover old forms of working, to maintain a diversity of organizational responses. Contemporary organization is designed to achieve quick wins; older varieties had useful attributes to do with stability, continuity, and loyalty. There are benefits to be had in maintaining such diversity in our social ecology.

While the need for responsiveness is always there, and you can never control for changes in a turbulent environment, this is not by itself a lot of help in thinking about the needs of vulnerable people having to live with their diminished capacity to be responsive to change.

Instead, what we are seeing is that the most vulnerable members of society have to live with the anxieties of those much more powerful than themselves. In thinking about societal dynamics, we may ask about these underlying anxieties that are being manifested in our social systems: does one size fit all? Or is there a fear aroused by the weak in the stronger, so that those who have most advantages in the way of social, psychological, and economic comforts are most threatened and afraid of losing their sense of personal security if they take notice of the needs of the unenterprising in an enterprise culture? The sad injustice of this is that the weak can live with being weak if we let them, but the anxieties of the more powerful continue to undermine further that capacity of the vulnerable to live life on their own terms.

A psychodynamic approach encourages a necessary insight into the importance of relational aspects of care. Looking at the systemic context allows us also to question why good practice is not so difficult to introduce but is less easy to maintain over time. This binocular perspective can make a contribution, therefore, to both the theory and the practice of care of vulnerable people. A working definition of a vulnerable person is one who through personality or circumstance is more vulnerable than we think is right in a stable and well-ordered world—more vulnerable than us, in effect. In the end, the worst disadvantage that the vulnerable have in relation to the rest of us is that by reminding us of their weakness they make us feel anxious and guilty about our need to get on with our lives. I feel so bad about not phoning my poor old aunt that I forget to phone her again today.

Notes

1. *The Guardian*, 18 June 2008, in an article to mark the 60th anniversary of the NHS.

2. Oral submission to the House of Commons Health Committee, November 2009.

3. *The Guardian*, 16 April 2008.

4. *The Guardian*, 25 November 2009.

5. I am grateful to a colleague, Tony McCaffrey, for this formulation of the primary task of health and social welfare teams.

REFERENCES

Age Concern (2006). *Hungry to Be Heard: The Scandal of Malnourished Older People in Hospital*. London: Age Concern England.

Alzheimer's Society (2009). *Counting the Cost: Caring for People with Dementia on Hospital Wards*. London: Alzheimer's Society.

Armstrong, D. (2005). *Organization in the Mind: Psychoanalysis, Group Relations, and Organizational Consultancy*. London: Karnac.

Athill, D. (2008). *Somewhere Towards the End*. London: Granta.

Badcock, C. (1986). *The Problem of Altruism*. Oxford: Blackwell.

Bair, D. (1978). *Samuel Beckett: A Biography*. London: Jonathan Cape.

Bate, J. (Ed.) (2004). *Selected Poetry of John Clare*. London: Faber & Faber.

Beckett, S. (1958). *Endgame*. In: *Samuel Beckett: The Complete Dramatic Works*. London: Faber & Faber, 1986.

Bertalanffy, L. von (1950). An outline of general system theory. *British Journal of Philosophy of Science*, 1: 134–165.

Bell, C., & Newby, M. (1972). *Community Studies: An Introduction to the Sociology of the Local Community*. London: George Allen & Unwin.

Bell, D. (1973). *Coming of Post-Industrial Society*. New York: Basic Books.

Bennett, A. (2005). *Untold Stories*. London: Faber & Faber.

Bion, W. R. (1961). *Experiences in Groups*. London: Routledge.

Bion, W. R. (1962). A theory of thinking. *International Journal of Psychoanalysis, 43*: 306–310. Reprinted in: *Second Thoughts: Selected Papers on Psychoanalysis* (pp. 110–119). London: Heinemann, 1967.

Bion, W. R. (1970). *Attention and Interpretation*. London: Tavistock Publications.

Bishop, J., & Hoggett, P. (1986). *Organizing around Enthusiasms: Mutual Aid in Leisure*. London: Comedia.

Bowlby, J. (1971). *Attachment and Loss*. London: Penguin.

Bruggen, P. (1997). *Who Cares? True Stories of the NHS Reforms*. Charlbury: Jon Carpenter.

Burton, J. (2007). Care homes: Do they "care" and are they "homes"? *Journal of Care Services Management, 1* (3): 221–232.

Campbell, D., Draper, R., & Huffington, C. (1991). *A Systemic Approach to Consultation*. London: Karnac .

Carr, W. (1996). Learning for leadership. *Leadership and Organization Development Journal, 17* (6): 46–52.

Carr, W. (2001). The exercise of authority in a dependent context. In: L. Gould, L. Stapley, & M. Stein (Eds.), *The Systems Psychodynamics of Organisations*. London: Karnac.

Committee of Public Accounts (2008). *Improving Services and Support for People with Dementia, Sixth Report of Session 2007–08*. London: House of Commons.

Cooper, A. (2007). *Is the (Post-war Bevanite) Welfare State Dead?* Tavistock Policy Seminar, June.

Cooper, A., & Dartington, T. (2004). The vanishing organization: Organizational containment in a networked world. In C. Huffington & D. Armstrong (Eds.), *Working Below the Surface: The Emotional Life of Contemporary Organizations* (pp. 127–150). London: Karnac.

Cooper, A., & Lousada, J. (2005). *Borderline Welfare: Feeling and Fear of Feeling in Modern Welfare*. London: Karnac.

CSCI (2005). *The State of Social Care in England 2004/05*. London: Commission for Social Care Inspection.

CSCI (2008). *The State of Social Care in England 2006/07*. London: Commission for Social Care Inspection.

Damasio, A. (1994). *Descartes' Error: Emotion, Reason and the Human Brain*. New York: Putnam.

Dartington, A. (1994). The significance of the outsider in families and other social groups. In: S. Box (Ed.), *Crisis at Adolescence: Object Relations Therapy with the Family*. Mahwah, NJ: Jason Aronson.

Dartington, A. (2007) (with Pratt, R.). My unfaithful brain. In: R. Davenhill (Ed.), *Looking into Later Life: A Psychoanalytic Approach to Depression and Dementia in Old Age* (pp. 283–297). London: Karnac.

Dartington, T. (1971). *Task Force*. London: Mitchell Beazley.

Dartington, T. (1978). *Volunteers and Psychiatric Aftercare*. Berkhamsted: Volunteer Centre, with MIND.

Dartington, T. (1979). Fragmentation and integration in health care: The referral process and social brokerage. *Sociology of Health and Illness, 1* (1): 12–39.

Dartington, T. (1980). *Family Care of Old People*. London: Souvenir Press.

Dartington, T. (1983). At home in hospital? In: M. Denham (Ed.), *Care of the Long-Stay Elderly Patient*. London: Croom Helm.

Dartington, T. (1986). *The Limits of Altruism: Elderly Mentally Infirm People as a Test Case for Collaboration*. London: King Edward's Hospital Fund for London.

Dartington, T. (1996). Leadership and management: Oedipal struggles in voluntary organisations. *Leadership & Organization Development Journal, 17* (6): 12–16.

Dartington, T. (1998). From altruism to action: Primary task and the not-for-profit organisation. *Human Relations, 51* (12): 1477–1493.

Dartington, T. (2001). The preoccupations of the citizen: Reflections from the OPUS Listening Posts. *Organisational and Social Dynamics, 1* (1): 94–112.

Dartington, T. (2004). In defence of inefficiency. *Organisational and Social Dynamics, 4* (2): 298–310.

Dartington, T. (2007). Two days in December. *Dementia, 6* (3): 327–341.

Dartington, T. (2008) (with Coupe, K., Malloy, L., Brennan, M., & Sampson, E.). Dying from dementia—a patient's journey. *British Medical Journal, 337*: 931–933.

Dartington, T. (2009). Relationship and dependency in the public sphere. *Soundings, 42*: 60–66.

Dartington, T., Henry, G., & Menzies Lyth, I. (1976). *The Psychological Welfare of Young Children Making Long Stays in Hospital*. London: Tavistock Institute, CASR Doc. 1200

Dartington, T., Jones, P., & Miller, E. (1974). *Geriatric Hospital Care*. London: Tavistock Institute, CASR Doc. 1051.

Dartington, T., Miller, E., & Gwynne, G. (1981). *A Life Together: The Distribution of Attitudes around the Disabled*. London: Tavistock Publications.

Davenhill, R. (Ed.) (2007a). *Looking into Later Life: A Psychoanalytic Approach to Depression and Dementia in Old Age*. London: Karnac.

Davenhill, R. (2007b). No truce with the Furies. In: R. Davenhill (Ed.), *Looking into Later Life: A Psychoanalytic Approach to Depression and Dementia in Old Age* (pp. 201–221). London: Karnac.

Davenhill, R., Balfour, A., & Rustin, M. (2007). Psychodynamic observation and old age. In: R. Davenhill (Ed.), *Looking into Later Life: A Psychoanalytic Approach to Depression and Dementia in Old Age* (pp. 129–144). London: Karnac.

Davison, N., & Williams, K. (2009). Compassion in nursing 1: Defining, identifying and measuring this essential quality. 2: Factors that influence compassionate care in clinical practice. *Nursing Times*, *105*: 35–36.

de Botton, A. (2000). *The Consolations of Philosophy*. Harmondsworth: Penguin.

de Botton. A. (2004). *Status Anxiety*. London: Hamish Hamilton.

Department of Health (2009). *Living Well with Dementia: A National Dementia Strategy*. London.

De Wacle, I., van Loon, J., Van Hove, G., & Schalock, R. (2005). Quality of life versus quality of care: Implications for people and programs. *Journal of Policy and Practice in Intellectual Disabilities, 2* (3–4): 229–239.

Douglas, M. (1966). *Purity and Danger: An Analysis of Concepts of Pollution and Taboo*. London: Routledge.

Duffy, S. (2005). Individual budgets: Transforming the allocation of resources for care. *Journal of Integrated Care, 13* (1).

Elder, G. (1977). *The Alienated: Growing Old Today*. London: Writers and Readers Publishing Cooperative.

Eliot, T. S. (1917). *The Love Song of J. Alfred Prufrock*. In: *Collected Poems*. London: Faber & Faber, 1963.

Emery, F., & Trist, E. (1965). The causal texture of organizational environments. *Human Relations, 18*: 21–32.

Evans, J. (2009). "As if" intimacy? Mediated persona, politics and gender. In: S. Day Schlater, D. Jones, H. Price, & C. Yates (Eds.), *Emotion: New Psychosocial Perspectives* (pp. 72–84). Basingstoke: Palgrave.

Evans, S. (2008). "Beyond forgetfulness": How psychoanalytic ideas can help us to understand the experience of patients with dementia. *Psychoanalytic Psychotherapy, 22* (3): 155–176.

Feldman, C. (2005). *Compassion: Listening to the Cries of the World.* Berkeley, CA: Rodmell Press.

Fotaki, M. (2006). Choice is yours: A psychodynamic exploration of health policymaking and its consequence for the English National Health Service. *Human Relations, 59* (12): 1711–1744.

Freud, S. (1895d). *Studies on Hysteria. Standard Edition, 2.*

Freud, S. (1912–13). *Totem and Taboo. Standard Edition, 13.*

Froggart, K., & Payne, S. (2006). A survey of end-of-life care in care homes: Issues of definition and practice. *Health and Social Care in the Community, 14* (4): 341–348.

Gabriel, Y. (1999). *Organizations in Depth.* London: Sage.

Garner, J. (2004). Dementia. In: E. Evans & J. Garner (Eds.), *Talking Over the Years.* Hove: Brunner-Routledge.

Glyn, A. (2006). *Capitalism Unleashed: Finance, Globalization, and Welfare.* Oxford: Oxford University Press.

Goodrich, J., & Cornwell, J. (2008). *Seeing the Person in the Patient: The Point of View Review Paper.* London: King's Fund.

Goodwin, N. (2007). Developing effective joint commissioning between health and social care: Prospects for the future based on lessons from the past. *Journal of Care Services Management, 1* (3): 279–293.

Gould, L., Stapley, L., & Stein, M. (2001). *The Systems Psychodynamics of Organizations.* London: Karnac.

Grotstein, J. (2007). *A Beam of Intense Darkness: Wilfred Bion's Legacy to Psychoanalysis.* London: Karnac.

Heidegger, M. (1927). *Being and Time.* Oxford: Blackwell, 1962.

Herzen, A. (1924). *My Past and Thoughts: The Memoirs of Alexander Herzen.* Berkeley, CA: University of California Press, 1992.

Hinshelwood, R., & Skogstad, W. (2000). *Observing Organisations: Anxiety, Defence and Culture in Health Care.* London: Routledge.

Hirschhorn, L. (1997). *Reworking Authority: Leading and Following in the Post-modern Organization.* Cambridge, MA: MIT Press.

HM Government (2009). *Shaping the Future of Care Together*. London. Cm. 7673.

Hoggart, R. (2005). *Promises to Keep: Thoughts in Old Age*. London: Continuum.

Hoggett, P. (1992). *Partisans in an Uncertain World: The Psychoanalysis of Engagement*. London: Free Association Books.

Hoggett, P., Beedell, P., Juminez, L., Mayo, M., & Miller, C. (2006). Identity, life history and commitment to welfare. *Journal of Social Policy, 35* (4): 689–704.

Holman, C. (2006). *Living Bereavement: An Exploration of Health Care Workers' Response to Loss and Grief in an NHS Continuing Care Ward for Older People*. PhD thesis, City University, London.

Hughes, J., Louw, S., & Sabat, S. (2006). *Dementia: Mind, Meaning, and the Person*. Oxford: Oxford University Press.

Hume, D. (1740). *A Treatise of Human Nature*. Oxford: Clarendon University Press, 1978.

James, A. (1994). *Managing to Care: Public Service and the Market*. London: Longman.

James, O. (2007). *Affluenza*. London: Ebury Press.

Jaques, E. (1951). *The Changing Culture of a Factory*. London: Tavistock.

Jaques, E. (1955). Social systems as a defence against persecutory and depressive anxiety. In: M. Klein, P. Heimann, & R. Money-Kyrle (Eds.), *New Directions in Psychoanalysis* (pp. 478–498). London: Tavistock Publications.

Jensen, M., & Meckling, W. (1998). The nature of man. In: M. Jensen, *Foundations of Organizational Strategy*. Cambridge, MA: Harvard University Press.

Jervis, S. (2009). The use of self as a research tool. In: S. Clarke & P. Hoggett (Eds.), *Researching Beneath the Surface: Psycho-Social Research Methods in Practice* (pp. 145–166). London: Karnac.

Jones, P., Dartington, T., Hilgendorf, L., & Irving, B. (1973). *Balderton Hospital Research Project*. London: Tavistock Institute, HRC/CASR doc. 907.

Jung, C. G. (1961). *Memories, Dreams, Reflections*. New York: Random House.

Juvenal (1992). *The Satires*, trans. N. Rudd. Oxford: Oxford University Press.

Kafka, F. (1925). *The Trial*. Harmondsworth: Penguin, 2007.

Kauffman, S. (1995). *At Home in the Universe: The Search for Laws of Complexity*. New York: Oxford University Press.

Keady, J., Ashcroft-Simpson, S., & Halligan, K. (2007). Admiral nursing and the family care of a parent with dementia: Using autobiographical narrative as grounding for negotiated clinical practice and decision-making. *Scandinavian Journal of Caring Science, 21*: 345–353.

Keenan, B. (1992). *An Evil Cradling*. London: Hutchinson.

Khaleelee, O., & Miller, E. (1985). Beyond the small group: Society as an intelligible field of study. In M. Pines (Ed.), *Bion and Group Psychotherapy*. London: Routledge & Kegan Paul.

Kitwood, T. (1997). *Dementia Reconsidered: The Person Comes First*. Buckingham: Open University Press.

Klein, M. (1926). The psychological principles of early analysis. *International Journal of Psychoanalysis, 8*: 25–37.

Klein, M. (1945). The Oedipus complex in the light of early anxieties. In: *Love, Guilt and Reparation and Other Works, 1921–1945* (pp. 370–419). London: Hogarth Press & the Institute of Psychoanalysis, 1975.

Klein, M. (1946). Notes on some schizoid mechanisms. In: *Envy and Gratitude and Other Works, 1946–1963* (pp. 1–24). London: Hogarth Press & the Institute of Psychoanalysis, 1980.

Lawrence, W. (1977). Management development: Some ideals, images and realities. *Journal of European Industrial Training, 1* (2): 21–25.

Lawrence, W. (1979). A concept for today: The management of oneself in role. In W. G. Lawrence (Ed.), *Exploring Individual and Organizational Boundaries* (pp. 235–249). Chichester: Wiley.

Lawrence, W. (2000). *Tongued with Fire: Groups in Experience*. London: Karnac.

Lawson, N. (1992). *The View from Number 11: Memoirs of a Tory Radical*. London: Bantam.

Layard, R. (2005). *Happiness: Lessons from a New Science*. Harmondsworth: Penguin.

Leadbetter, C. (2004). *Personalisation through Participation: A New Script for Public Services*. London: Demos.

Leat, D. (1988). *Voluntary Organisations and Accountability*. London: National Council for Voluntary Organisations.

Lewin, K. (1947). Frontiers in group dynamics. *Human Relations, 1* (1): 5–41; *1* (2): 143–153

Lipsky, M. (1980). *Street-level Bureaucracy: Dilemmas of the Individual in Public Services*. New York: Russell Sage Foundation.

Locke, J. (1690). *An Essay Concerning Human Understanding*. Oxford: Clarendon University Press, 1975.

Long, S. (2008). *The Perverse Organization and Its Deadly Sins*. London: Karnac.

MacIntyre, A. (1981). *After Virtue: A Study in Moral Theory* (3rd edition). London: Duckworth, 2007.

Malloy, L. (2009). Thinking about dementia—a psychodynamic understanding of links between early infantile experience and dementia. *Psychoanalytic Psychotherapy, 23* (2): 109–120.

Markillie, R. (2007). The experience of an illness: The resurrection of an analysis in the work of recovery In: R. Davenhill (Ed.), *Looking into Later Life: A Psychoanalytic Approach to Depression and Dementia in Old Age* (pp. 108–126). London: Karnac.

Marriott, H. (2003). *The Selfish Pig's Guide to Caring*. Clifton: Polperro Heritage Press.

Marris, P. (1996). *The Politics of Uncertainty: Attachment in Private and Public Life*. London: Routledge.

Maslow, A. (1970). *Motivation and Personality*. New York: Harper & Row.

Matthews, E. (2002). *The Philosophy of Merleau-Ponty*. Chesham: Acumen.

McGregor, D. (1960). *The Human Side of Enterprise*. New York: McGraw-Hill.

Meltzer, D., & Harris, M. (1976). A psycho-analytic model of the child-in-the-family-in-the-community. In: *Sincerity and Other Works: Collected Papers of Donald Meltzer*, ed. A. Hahn. London: Karnac, 1984

Menzies Lyth, I. (1960). The functioning of social systems as a defence against anxiety. In: *Containing Anxiety in Institutions: Selected Essays* (pp. 43–85). London: Free Association Books, 1988.

Menzies Lyth, I. (1973). Action research in a long-stay hospital. In: *Containing Anxiety in Institutions: Selected Essays* (pp. 130–207). London: Free Association Books, 1988.

Menzies Lyth, I. (1979). Staff support systems: Task and anti-task in adolescent institutions. In: *Containing Anxiety in Institutions: Selected Essays* (pp. 222–235). London: Free Association Books, 1988.

Meyer, J., Ashburner, C., & Holman, C. (2006). Becoming connected, being caring. *Educational Action Research, 14* (4): 477–496.

Miller, E. (1975). Socio-technical systems in weaving, 1953–1970: A follow-up study. *Human Relations, 28*: 349–386.

Miller, E. (Ed.) (1976). *Task and Organisation.* Chichester: Wiley.

Miller, E. (1979). Autonomy, dependency and organizational change. In: D. Towell & C. Harries (Eds.), *Innovation in Patient Care* (pp. 172–190). London: Croom Helm.

Miller, E. (1989). Experiential learning in groups. I: The development of the Leicester model; II: Recent developments in dissemination and application. In: E. Trist & H. Murray (Eds.), *The Social Engagement of Social Science: A Tavistock Anthology. Vol. 1: The Socio-Psychological Perspective* (pp. 165–198). Philadelphia, PA: University of Pennsylvania, 1990.

Miller, E. (1993a). *From Dependency to Autonomy: Studies in Organization and Change.* London: Free Association Books.

Miller, E. (1993b). Geriatric hospitals as open systems. In: *From Dependency to Autonomy: Studies in Organization and Change* (pp. 82–98). London: Free Association Books.

Miller, E. J., & Gwynne, G. V. (1972). *A Life Apart: A Pilot Study of Residential Institutions for the Physically Handicapped and the Young Chronic Sick.* London: Tavistock Publications.

Miller, E. J., & Rice, A. K. (1967). *Systems of Organization: Task and Sentient Systems and Their Boundary Control.* London: Tavistock Publications.

National Audit Office (2007). *Improving Services and Support for People with Dementia.* London: The Stationery Office.

Neumann, J. (1999). Systems psychodynamics in the service of political organizational change. In: R. French & R. Vince (Eds.), *Group Relations, Management, and Organization* (pp. 54–69). Oxford: Oxford University Press.

Nicholson, C. (2009). *Holding It Together: A Psycho-Social Exploration of Living with Frailty in Old Age.* PhD thesis, City University, London.

Nolan, J. (1998). *The Therapeutic State: Justifying Government at Century's End.* New York: New York University Press.

Nuffield Council on Bioethics (2009). *Dementia: Ethical Issues.* London.

Obholzer, A. (1994). Managing social anxieties in public sector organizations. In A. Obholzer & V. Roberts (Eds.), *The Unconscious at Work: Individual and Organizational Stress in the Human Services* (pp. 169–178). London: Routledge.

Obholzer, A., & Roberts, V. (1994). *The Unconscious at Work: Individual and Organizational Stress in the Human Services*. London: Routledge.

Palmer, B. (2002). Stroke. In: *Always the Sea*. Aberystwyth: Annwn Books.

Pattison, S., & Paton, R. (1997). The religious dimensions of management belief. *Iconoclastic Papers, 1* (1).

Peters, T. (1989). *Thriving on Chaos*. London: Macmillan.

Pollock, A. (2004). *NHS plc: The Privatization of Our Health Care*. London: Verso.

Putnam, R. (2000). *Bowling Alone: The Collapse and Revival of American Community*. New York: Simon & Schuster.

Reiff, P. (1966). *The Triumph of the Therapeutic*. New York: Harper & Row.

Rice, A. K. (1958). *Productivity and Social Organization: The Ahmadabad Experiment*. London: Tavistock.

Rice, A. K. (1965). *Learning for Leadership*. London: Tavistock.

Robb, B. (1967). *Sans Everything: A Case to Answer*. London: Nelson.

Roberts, V. (1994). The self-assigned impossible task. In: A. Obholzer & V. Roberts (Eds.), *The Unconscious at Work: Individual and Organizational Stress in the Human Services*. London: Routledge.

Rose, G. (1985). *Love's Work*. London: Chatto & Windus.

Rosenfeld, H. (1971). A clinical approach to the psychoanalytic theory of the life and death instincts: An investigation into the aggressive aspects of narcissism. In: E. Bott Spillius (Ed.), *Melanie Klein Today: Developments in Theory and Practice. Vol. 1: Mainly Theory* (pp. 239–255). London: Routledge, 1988.

Roth, P. (2006). *Everyman*. London: Jonathan Cape.

Royal Commission on Long Term Care (1999). *With Respect to Old Age: Long Term Care—Rights and Responsibilities* (The Sutherland Report). London: The Stationery Office, Cm 4192.

Royal Society of Arts (1995). *Tomorrow's Company*. RSA Inquiry Report. Aldershot: Gower.

Rustin, M., & Bradley, J. (Eds.) (2008). *Work Discussion: Learning from Reflective Practice in Work with Children and Families*. London: Karnac.

Sampson, E., Harrison-Dening, K., Greenish, W., Mandal, U., Holman, A., & Jones, L. (2009). *End of Life Care for People with Dementia*. London: Marie Curie Cancer Care.

Savage, B., Widdowson, T., & Wright, T. (1979). Improving the care of the elderly. In: D. Towell & C. Harries (Eds.), *Innovation in Patient Care* (pp. 61–81). London: Croom Helm.

Schon, D. (1971). *Beyond the Stable State*. London: Temple Smith.

Segal, H. (1986). Fear of death: Note on the analysis of an old man. In: *The Work of Hannah Segal: A Kleinian Approach to Clinical Practice* (pp. 173–182). London: Free Association Books.

Sennett, R. (1977). *The Fall of Public Man*. London: Faber & Faber.

Sennett, R. (1998). *The Corrosion of Character: The Personal Consequences of Work in the New Capitalism*. New York: Norton.

Shapiro, E., & Carr, W. (1991). *Lost in Familiar Places*. New Haven, CT: Yale University Press.

Sinason, V. (1992). The man who was losing his brain. In: *Mental Handicap and the Human Condition: New Approaches from the Tavistock*. London: Free Association Books.

Smiles, S. (1859). *Self-Help*. Oxford: Oxford University Press, 2002.

Smith, R. (2000). A good death. *British Medical Journal*, 320: 129–130.

Snowdon, D. (2001). *Ageing with Grace: The Nun Study and the Science of Old Age*. London: Fourth Estate.

Sofer, C. (1961). *The Organisation from Within*. London: Tavistock.

Sontag, S. (1978). *Illness as Metaphor*. New York: Farrar, Strauss & Giraux; reprinted Harmondsworth: Penguin, 2002.

Stacey, R. (1996). *Complexity and Creativity in Organizations*. San Francisco: Berrett-Koehler.

Stein, M. (2007). Toxicity and the unconscious experience of the body at the employee–customer interface. *Organization Studies*, 8: 1223–1241.

Steiner, J. (1987). The interplay between pathological organisations and the paranoid-schizoid and depressive positions. In: E. Bott Spillius (Ed.), *Melanie Klein Today: Developments in Theory and Practice. Vol. 1: Mainly Theory*. London: Routledge, 1988.

Suttie, I. (1935). *The Origins of Love and Hate*. London: Kegan Paul, Trench Trübner.

Symington, N. (1994). *Emotion and Spirit*. London: Karnac, 1998.

Taylor, F. E. (1947). *Scientific Management*. New York: Harper & Row.

Terry, P. (2006). *What the Hell, She's Going to Die Anyway—Ageism and*

Projective Identification. Symposium paper for the BPsS Psychology Specialists Working with Older People Conference.

Thomas, R. S. (2004). Geriatric. In: *Collected Later Poems 1988–2000*. Tarset: Bloodaxe Books.

Towell, D. (1975). *Understanding Psychiatric Nursing*. London: Royal College of Nursing.

Towell, D., & Harries, C. (Eds.) (1979). *Innovation in Patient Care*. London: Croom Helm.

Trist, E., & Bamforth, K. (1951). Some social and psychological consequences of the longwall method of coal-getting. *Human Relations*, 4: 3–38.

Waddell, M. (2002). *Inside Lives: Psychoanalysis and the Growth of the Personality* (2nd edition). London: Karnac.

Walshe, K. (2003). *Regulating Healthcare: A Prescription for Improvement?* Maidenhead: Open University Press.

Wanless, D., Appelby, J., Harrison, A., & Patel, D. (2007). *Our Future Health Secured? A Review of NHS Funding and Performance*. London: King's Fund.

Whitman, L. (2009). *Telling Tales about Dementia: Experiences of Caring*. London: Jessica Kingsley.

Wilkinson, R., & Pickett, K. (2009). *The Spirit Level: Why More Equal Societies Almost Always Do Better*. London: Allen Lane.

Winnicott, D. (1965). *The Maturational Processes and the Facilitating Environment*. London: Karnac, 1990.

Zeldin, T. (1994). *An Intimate History of Humanity*. London: Sinclair-Stevenson.